FAQs

Biblical answers to youth and children's leaders' questions

Edited by Alison Mitchell

THE GOOD BOOK COMPANY

FAQs: Biblical answers to youth and children's leaders' questions

© The Good Book Company 2006

Published by The Good Book Company
Elm House, 37 Elm Road, New Malden, Surrey KT3 3HB
Tel: 0845-225-0880; Fax: 0845-225-0990
E-mail: admin@thegoodbook.co.uk
website: www.thegoodbook.co.uk

ISBN: 1-905564-45-7
ISBN 13: 978-1-905564-45-3

Cover design by Carl Hamblin. Illustrations by André Parker.
Printed in the UK by Bookmarque

Contents

What are your FAQs?

EVERY YOUTH GROUP, Sunday school or club is unique. Different leaders, with different personalities and gifts. Different members with varied social, ethnic and religious backgrounds. And different styles of churches. But as we have travelled round the country over the last eight years running training events for local leaders, we have found a consistent pattern has emerged in the questions that they most frequently wrestle with.

At these *Big Issue** training events, we have been championing an approach to youth and children's work that we describe as 'Bible-centred.' What we mean by this phrase is that we want the teaching of God's Word, the Bible, not only to provide the *content* of what we try to communicate to the young people in our care, but also to provide the *priorities* of what we

---

* For further information about The Big Issue training events see the appendix on page 156.

expend our energies on, and to underpin the whole *philosophy* of what a group does when it meets together.

We believe that the hearing of God's Word, as it is carefully and faithfully taught, should be the central thing on the agenda whenever a group meets. That is what we mean by Bible-centred.

So we asked experienced youth and children's leaders who share our approach to give their considered answers to the top ten frequently asked questions (FAQs), based on their study of Scripture, and their long experience in dealing with these issues on a weekly basis. The result is, we hope and pray, a book that you will not simply read and forget, but an ongoing resource that you will reflect on, re-read and use to shape the content, style and practicalities of the ministry you are involved in.

The opening chapter by Ian Fry is foundational in understanding the rest of the book. So although you may be tempted to flip straight away to the question that is uppermost in your mind, can we urge you to take the time to read this opening chapter thoughtfully, carefully and prayerfully, as it sets the framework for everything that follows?

It is our prayer that this practical handbook will help you to do gospel ministry that is pleasing to God our Father, brings glory to His Son, our Saviour, is filled with the Spirit's power, and bears fruit that will last to all eternity.

Alison Mitchell
October 2006

1. What's it all about?

What is Christian youth work?

> The generation that knows only itself is destined to remain adolescent forever.*

AT THE RISK of gross understatement, the church scene today has a huge focus on youth and children's work. In some ways, it is continuing in a proud tradition of caring for young people, and yet in others, it is a departure from the past. The more obvious developments are:

- a vast array of para-church organisations involved in ministering to the young;

- training courses of all types offering support, guidance and qualifications;

- full-time youth workers becoming the 'norm'.

Given this, it is important to ask the question, 'What is Christian youth work?' The vast amount of time, thinking and

---

*Mark DeVries. Family-Based Youth Ministry.

effort expended among the young means that this is a vitally important question.

In order to provide an answer that avoids over reliance on pragmatism, we need to start with the Bible. Yet right away, we discover that this is not as straightforward as it seems. For a start, you look in vain for the role of youth worker: it has been noted that the only example of someone, besides parents, working with a young person is Eli with Samuel, which is a fascinating model for ministry! How are we to respond to issues such as this?

It is important to survey what the Bible does have to say generally about children and young people, before turning to the detail. There are seven biblical points we need to consider:

1. God says that the prime responsibility for the spiritual nurture of children and adolescents lies with parents

Time after time in the Old Testament, we see the role of family as central to God's plans and purposes:

- **Exodus 20 v 12:** God places people in families and expects those relationships to be honoured.

- **Proverbs 1 v 8:** It is the job of families to pass on God's truth, with both parents involved in the teaching process.

- **Genesis 18 v 19 and Proverbs 1 – 9:** The prime responsibility however falls to the father, whose task is to teach so that the young person will be wise, not merely have a head full of knowledge.

- **Proverbs 4 v 23; 23 v 26:** The heart is the focus for the father.

- **Proverbs 4 v 1-2** shows that the parent has authority and that this authority derives from the wisdom which has been learned from their own parents. (Proverbs 4 v 3-9).

- **Proverbs 4 v 10–19** further shows the parent acting as a guide, encouraging the learner to reasonable action through persuasion, not just coercion.

Clearly, the role of guide is something that develops as the child progresses through to adolescence, so that in the teen years the parent is walking alongside their child as they begin to move to independence. Throughout, though, the parent endeavours to speed up the learning process and to prevent unnecessary and perhaps painful detours by the learner.

In the New Testament the focus on parental responsibility continues:

- **Ephesians 6 v 1-3; Colossians 3 v 20:** These are the only verses directed to children, and these see them in their family relationships.

- **2 Timothy 1 v 5:** The immense impact of a godly home in Timothy's case is noted. (In his case, it is the godly teaching of his mother and grandmother that is mentioned.)

2. God desires that learning is always with the aim of living for His glory

Any overview of biblical teaching shows this emphasis throughout Scripture. So, for example, Psalm 78 declares that the aim of teaching 'the praiseworthy deeds of the LORD' (v 4) is that 'the next generation would know them' (v 6).

In a sermon on this psalm, John Piper states:

> The aim of all true education is to deepen and broaden confidence in God. This is what keeps learning from leading to pride—or should keep learning from leading to pride. All true learning, all true knowledge, reveals that we are dependent on God and must depend on Him or perish. *Knowledge that leads to self-sufficiency rather than dependence on God is not true knowledge but flawed knowledge.* It is like an archaeologist who finds a beautiful ancient painting, but hides it in a locked case and travels around giving lectures on how clever he was to discover it, but never bringing it out for all to admire, lest the beauty of the original treasure detract from his own achievement in finding it.*

---

* John Piper. Raising children who are confident in God. Sermon. Bethlehem Baptist Church. February 1996. Emphasis mine.

3. God demands that learning occurs as part of life

Deuteronomy 6 v 6-9 and **11 v 18-21** make fascinating reading. They show that the entire world and its ways were to be explained through the lens of Scripture. The child and young person thus learned that the whole of life fell under God's control: the sacred/secular divide did not exist. God and His ways were applied throughout life, and were expected to be seen beyond the special religious gatherings of God's people. God was to be at the centre of everything.

John Piper puts it well:

> If there is one memory that our children should have of our families and our church it is this; they should remember God. God was first. God was central. There was a passion for the supremacy of God in all things.*

Both Jesus and Paul, although not working specifically with children or young people, adopted this model of ministry. In Acts 4 v 13 it was noted that the disciples 'had been *with* Jesus', while Paul talks about the intensity of relationship he had with the Christians at Thessalonica (1 Thessalonians 2 v 8).

Relationship was therefore key to the learning process. The modern distinction we make between knowledge and life did not exist. Indeed, the Jewish idea of learning meant that what went on in the mind was inseparably linked to what went on in the body—education was meant to address the whole person. Education in the things of God was meant to lead to exultation in God.

---

* John Piper. Raising children who are confident in God. Sermon. Bethlehem Baptist Church. February 1996.

Mark Ashton, in his classic book *Christian Youth Work*, put it like this:

> In the West we are accustomed to think of the 'truth' as a disembodied abstract. The Bible does not see it in this way. When Pilate asked his question, 'What is truth?' Jesus had already provided the answer: 'I am the way, the truth, and the life.' The biblical measure of truth is the person of Jesus Christ. Truth in the Bible is a quality of persons, primarily, and of propositions only secondarily. So the communication of that truth is from one whole person to another whole person. It is less than the whole truth if it involves less than the whole person.*

4. God's pattern sees children and young people worshipping as part of His people

It is striking just how many times we read of children being part of corporate worship.

- **Exodus 12 v 26-27:**
  Whenever Passover occurred, children were present;

- **Deuteronomy 29 v 11-15:** When Israel entered into God's covenant, they were there;

- **Deuteronomy 31 v 10-12:** They were present at feast times;

- **2 Chronicles 20 v 5-13:** At times of seeking God, they were there.

Indeed, it was expected that acts of corporate worship would arouse the interest of, and provoke questioning by, children— see **Exodus 13 v 11-14.**

---

* Mark Ashton. *Christian Youth Work*. Authentic Media. 2006.

It seems that whenever the people of God gathered for corporate worship, the children and young people were present. And this practice was repeated in the early church:

• **Ephesians 6 v 1-4; Colossians 3 v 23:** As Paul wrote his letters to a number of churches, he had instructions for the children to follow. Specifically, having dealt with marital matters, Paul turned next to the children whom he expected to be present as his letter was read out. Imagine children listening to Ephesians chapters 1-4!

5. God does great things with young people

There are a large number of examples of young men and women who had a passionate love for God, that overflowed in sacrificial service for Him and His people.

• **Numbers 11 v 28:** As a youth, Joshua became Moses' assistant;

• **Jeremiah 1 v 5-7:** God appeared to and commissioned Jeremiah while he was a youth;

• **Joshua 6 v 23:** Young men carried out dangerous military missions;

- **1 Samuel 17 v 33:** The young shepherd boy David fought in the name of, and for the glory of, God.

- **Acts 23 v 16-22** records the actions of a young man fulfilling God's purposes.

Elsewhere we read of the likes of Joseph, Samuel, Samson, Joash, Azariah/Uzziah, Josiah, Esther, Daniel, Hananiah and Mishael, all of whom were entrusted with significant responsibility.

The adolescent years, then, were a time for great exploits for God. It's hard to escape the impression that biblical 'youth' does not even come close to the concept of 21st century adolescence. Ashton has got it exactly right when he says:

> We must not underestimate the spiritual experience and the spiritual potential of the teenager. *The Bible suggests that youth is made for heroism.* It is the world that insists it is made for pleasure... Are we sometimes guilty, not of asking too much, but of asking too little of teenagers, and so selling them and God short?*

6. A heart for God is essential

We have already seen that Deuteronomy 6 v 6-9 contains strong encouragement to teach through life. But it presupposes that the 'teacher' loves God deeply (v 5) and loves the truth of God: the commandments are to be on their hearts (v 6).

Statements of truth about God and commands from Him [propositions], far from being distant facts, are embraced by the teacher. His or her life is shaped by them so that their teaching is an overflow of a deep relationship with God.

---

* *Christian Youth Work.* Emphasis mine.

The first condition for any passing on of God's truth is a deep, continuing, daily, dependent walk with Almighty God. If we are not deeply passionate about God, we cannot expect our children and young people to be. It has been said that 'We copy those we admire'. Let us give them a God who is worth admiring.'

7. Adolescence as a concept

The category of 'youth' or 'adolescent', while clearly present in Scripture, does not have a definite age range or translate easily to modern conceptions of adolescence. While **Leviticus 27 v 2-3** may set 20 as the age when adulthood began, and the New Testament letters address young men as distinct categories, we have to note that the biblical view of 'youth' is very different from our conceptions of adolescence. Youth included those who were warriors and husbands and who, therefore, carried responsibility in the community.

Given a high view of the Bible as God's revealed Word, this should give us more than a little pause for thought. We know that adolescence, as a concept, is historically a recent phenomenon, which began midway through the 20th century. We also know that the effect of this has been to delay maturity in young people well into the 20's (and some cultural commentators are suggesting that it is being delayed still further into some people's 30's). For example, a recent article in *Time Magazine* observed:

> Social scientists are starting to realise that a permanent shift has taken place in the way we live our lives. In the past, people moved from childhood to adolescence and from adolescence to adulthood, but today there is a new, intermediate phase along the way. The years from 18 until 25 and even beyond have

become a distinct and separate life stage, a strange, transitional never-never land between adolescence and adulthood in which people stall for a few extra years, putting off the iron cage of adult responsibility that constantly threatens to crash down on them.*

We need to think carefully about the way we view adolescence, in case we unthinkingly buy into our culture in such a way that young people live down to low expectations of them. It is quite possible for us to expect them to be immature and to behave immaturely, and then find, unsurprisingly, that they respond accordingly. It is ironic that our culture effectively restrains maturity at the same time as it permits and encourages minimal restraint in key areas of conduct and thought such as alcohol consumption, sexual behaviour and the work ethic. Of course, young people are prone to large mood swings and immature thinking, but maybe we need to start thinking of the teen years more in terms of apprenticeship for adulthood rather than a time of freedom to 'discover their true identity'.

---

* Grossman, Lev 'Grow Up? Not So Fast.' *Time Magazine*, Vol. 165 No. 4, January 24, 2005

Implications

So what are we to make of the absence of youth workers in the Bible? Well, it does not mean that there should be no such role in our churches. But it does mean that this role should reflect the principles laid down in Scripture and operate accordingly. There are a clear number of implications from this biblical overview:

1. Christian youth work involves partnering with parents

The notion that young people are 'handed over' by parents for the children's and youth leaders to evangelise and nurture 'in church' must be resisted. At the very least, youth workers are to supplement what parents are modelling and teaching in the home. At the very best, youth leaders gifted by God to teach adolescents will be rendering vital assistance to parents in their God-given responsibility.

This also raises important questions about working amongst youngsters from pagan homes—something of huge importance, but which is too large to deal with in such a brief space. However, one thing needs to be noted. At the risk of generalising, it is still vital that we try to reinforce the family unit, except in obvious cases of neglect and abuse (though even here, surely our goal is to see young people saved and then loving their lost parents as Jesus loved those who are perishing).

2. Christian youth work involves teaching about God

In a postmodern (or ultramodern) culture, the attack on absolute and objective truth has seeped into Christian thinking and has led to a lack of confidence to teach the whole Bible.

Yet we should be able to say Paul's words to our young people:

I did not shrink from declaring to you the whole counsel of God.

Acts 20 v 27 (ESV)

3. *Christian youth work involves modelling and mentoring*

I suspect that some of the loss of confidence in teaching the whole Bible has been driven, not merely by contemporary cultural trends, but also by experiencing Bible teaching poorly done, all too often with little regard for the young person, and with poor relationship skills being displayed by the Bible-teaching youth worker. Yet relationship building is not optional—it is integral to Christian youth work. Time spent with young people is important if mentoring and modelling are to occur.

4. *Christian youth work involves integration with the community of God's people*

The popular concept that young people are best served by enjoying virtually exclusive contact with their peers while at church needs rethinking. The effective isolation of children and young people into peer groups means that their identity ends up being significantly shaped by the peer group. Niche-led approaches to youth ministry [eg: youth churches] are unhelpful because, by encouraging minimal or insignificant contact with mature adults, there is the distinct possibility that young people will not grow up as quickly as they could or should. Our aim must be to facilitate relationships across the age range of the church and encourage youngsters to see their parents as gifts from God. Exposure to the life and gatherings of the rest of the church are essential, not optional.

5. Christian youth work has high spiritual expectations

The lesson from Scripture is clear: we are to have high expectations of what God can do in a young life. God can and does expect to work in the lives of the young. Among the fruit of God's work will be a respect for parents and a desire to know the truth of the Bible in order that they may love God more.

There is a clear choice here: we either allow our ministry to be shaped by culture or we seek to be truly counter-cultural. Just as pastors and teachers, the youth worker's task is to prepare their young people to serve Christ, one aspect of which will surely be evangelising their peers (Ephesians 4 v 11-12).

6. Christian youth work needs to be led by the experienced and the godly

The assumption that only the young can reach the young must be questioned. If youth work involves a partnership with parents, then experience is vital so that parents are genuinely supported in their relationships with their children rather than, as can often happen, the youth worker interposing him or herself between the youngster and parents.

But alongside experience, it is vital that those in youth ministry have hearts full of God's Word and therefore full of God. This is not to say that younger Christians cannot be involved in some way or another—far from it. It is to ensure that any team of youth workers has godly and wise leadership.

Conclusions

I want now to give a definition of what I believe Christian youth work is:

> Christian Youth Work involves one generation, who know and love God from the heart, passing to the next generation the great truths of God, so that they in turn might find their joy in knowing, serving and loving Him and passing the truths of God on to the next generation (Psalm 78 v 1-8).

Where this is followed, we will not be satisfied with mere numbers attending meetings. We will aim for the following:

- young people who, out of a deep relationship with God through Christ, will love God deeply;

- young people for whom love for God is supreme, so that the world in which they are living will not prove alluring;

- young people for whom service to the Lord Jesus Christ is a natural outpouring of their love for Him;

- young people for whom daily death to self is an ongoing experience that they have as they are led by the Spirit of God;

- young people whose hearts are so gripped with the gospel that they want to see their friends [and enemies] saved for Christ.

Ian Fry lectures in youth and children's work at Oak Hill college. He's been involved in youth work in church settings, schools work, camps and houseparties for more years than he can remember. He is married to Nina and has three children.

Bible Study
Read Psalm 78 v 1-8

1. Who is the source of what we are to teach the next generation? (v 5) (The word 'law' here = 'teaching'.)

2. Who has Asaph learned about God from? (v 3)

3. What is to be the content of our teaching? (See how he describes God's work—this is not the language of cold detachment.) (v 4b)

4. How many generations are involved here? (v 5-6)

5. What is the great goal of our teaching? (Note this is relational language.) (v 7a)

6. When young people 'set their hope in God' how do they behave? (v 7b)

7. If young people do not 'set their hope in God' how will they behave? (v 8)

Applications:
• What have you learned from this study?

• How are you going to put this into practice in your ministry?

2. Desperately seeking leaders

What are the criteria for good children's and youth leaders?

EVERY FOUR YEARS the Olympics come round and the world's best athletes compete for their country. To get into the team they have to train hard and reach a certain standard in their discipline. Occasionally, a high-profile athlete will have an off day during the trials and they don't make the grade. They are left out of the team.

How did your team of youth and children's leaders end up like it is? Were there 'Olympic trials'? Perhaps some people couldn't think of an excuse fast enough to say 'No'. Maybe they are there grudgingly because no one else will do it. Or is it an excuse to get out of church and skip engaging with the sermon?

However it happened, the team of leaders is crucial to the children's and youth work. We must make sure that our young people are served as well as possible. But building the team is a tough job. In this chapter we will consider the criteria for good youth and children's leaders.

Let's start with what the Bible says:

Love God

> They chose Stephen, a man full of faith and of the Holy Spirit;
> Acts 6 v 5

In the early part of Acts we see the number of people being converted growing extremely fast. It must have been exciting. It becomes obvious that a larger team is needed, so in chapter 6 we have an account of how the first church did its team building. The criteria are of interest to us. The list doesn't include skills and gifts, although we will see that these things are important elsewhere. What matters is the individual's personal relationship with the Lord.

Stephen obviously stands out from the others and chapter 7 will be his chapter. Chapter 6 v 3, 5 and 8 tell us about him. He is full of the Spirit, wisdom, faith, God's grace and power. In our modern parlance, he is a 'full-on' Christian. Now, some of these characteristics are hard to judge. We certainly won't have many people quite like Stephen in our church. But there are some parallels for our leaders—they must be clearly converted, living fully for God. Their love for God must be obvious in their speech and actions. Their faith must be more than a hobby.

Hold the message firmly

> He must hold firmly to the trustworthy message as it has been taught, so that he can encourage others by sound doctrine and refute those who oppose it. **Titus 1 v 9**

It sounds like stating the obvious but it is fundamental that the leader accept the gospel. This has to be clear in his or her life and we should see a desire to dig deeper into God's Word and apply it personally. In their teaching they ought to use the Bible clearly to encourage and challenge others.

What the leader teaches must be 'sound'. In other words, it must be in line with what the Bible teaches as a whole and not contrary to the rest of the church. Young people's work is not the place for new things to arise. There is no place for the person who wants to 'do it my way'. The criterion here must be that the leader wants to do things God's way. In other words, they must love the gospel.

Public and Private Conduct

> Now the overseer must be above reproach, the husband of but one wife, temperate, self-controlled, respectable, hospitable, able to teach, not given to drunkenness, not violent but gentle, not quarrelsome, not a lover of money. He must manage his own family well and see that his children obey him with proper respect. **1 Timothy 3 v 2-4**

Paul adds 'not ... a recent convert' and 'have a good reputation with outsiders' a little later (1 Timothy 3 v 6, 7). We should remember that Paul is writing to Timothy and advising him about choosing leaders in the church. Before we jump to conclusions, we must recognise that these are high-profile, adult leadership roles. But the implications are the same for someone who is going to lead children or young people in their faith. Young people learn a lot by copying. They will copy the conduct and lifestyle of their Christian leaders. So those Christian leaders have to be above reproach in everything they do.

Some of those traits listed above are very appropriate for youth and children's leaders. Being temperate and self-controlled is crucial in an environment full of stresses. Being able to teach seems obvious, but note how often one sees someone 'good with the kids' unable to engage them and put across even simple Bible stories. Being hospitable is important especially in teenage work. If young people have access to our front room they will see our faith in action. They should be able to see how a Christian family works (by 'managing his own family well'), which they otherwise may never do. The young people should see the gospel teaching authenticated in a shared life.

Love God's people

> I thank my God every time I remember you... It is right for me to feel this way about all of you since I have you in my heart.
> **Philippians 1 v 3, 7**

As well as in his writing, Paul himself gives us a good example to follow. He is passionate about the gospel and passionate about passing it on to people. He is always praying for those he has ministered to. He writes and tells them this. He often prays for Christians that he has not met, but has heard of. In short, he loves other Christians.

We have all seen, at some stage, a school teacher, or someone else involved with young people, who obviously does not like them. That situation can make us cringe, or more likely worry, especially if we are parents. Youth and children's leaders should love the young people they are involved with. They should pray for them, enjoy their company and want the (gospel) best for them. Leaders should be willing to engage with the young people, sometimes being available to counsel them.

Love Teaching

Preach the Word; be prepared in season and out of season; correct, rebuke and encourage—with great patience and careful instruction. **2 Timothy 4 v 2**

Paul's charge to Timothy, as Paul himself approached the end of his ministry and life, is a much-quoted text. But it is much quoted because it is important. It neatly summarises the job of a church leader and evangelist. We have seen how our leaders must be converted, godly and biblical people with a heart for children or young people. Finally our leaders must love to teach.

There is no motivation, other than a huge desire to see young people get to grips with the Bible, that will work when it is 'out of season'. We all know what being 'out of season' means. Our leaders are ill or under pressure from their weekday job; the young people are going through a patch of ill discipline and rebellion against teaching; the hall that you use is being shared for that day with another even noisier group, and on top of that, the grass is being cut outside the windows, but it is too hot to close them. When it gets to quitting point, it is our leaders' love for teaching the Bible to children and young people that will get them through.

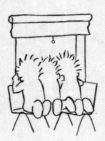

What does good practice look like?

There is much more that the Bible has to say about leadership. There are many good examples to follow and awful examples to avoid. The question remains: *how do we achieve good practice in Bible-based youthwork?* Do we ask youth and children's leaders to make an application alongside their Criminal Records check? This is rather a formal approach and may send out the wrong message about the task. Perhaps an informal interview with a church staff member and another volunteer (possibly the team leader) is appropriate. However you choose to appoint, do it carefully—having some sort of selection process is important. A practical idea for those occasions when the wrong person is on the team, is to start with a probationary period, although you probably wouldn't call it that. After six months you have a built-in opportunity to review alongside that leader.

In some cases, it may be wise to design a job description and ask potential leaders to accept it, possibly along with a doctrinal statement. This certainly allows the right questions to be asked at the right time. Going through the job description and doctrinal statements gives a context for an informal interview.

On the following page there are some suggestions for the shape of a possible job description—it is not meant to be exhaustive but to give a general idea. It does add in some practical aspects of good practice in youthwork that help to apply the biblical model of leadership outlined above.

Conclusion

We all know the people in our churches who we would like to sign up for the youth and children's work. However, the dream team usually remains just a dream! There are many other things to do in church life, even though many of the good people do several jobs. We have set a high standard in this chapter for our potential leaders and helpers. This is deliberate. We need quality Bible teachers and committed, gifted leaders right across the age groups. If your church leaders disagree with you make them read this book! Having said all that, we rarely get the team we desire. Is any of this worth it then?

SAMPLE JOB DESCRIPTION

Aims

Include on the job description a statement of the overall aim of the youth and children's work. Eg: 'to see children and young people come to know Jesus as Saviour and Lord and grow in that knowledge'. Remind the leaders that their ministry will have lifelong effects, as it says in Hebrews 13 v 7:

> *Remember your leaders, who spoke the word of God to you. Consider the outcome of their way of life and imitate their faith.*

Responsibilities

- To implement (or support) the faithful teaching of the Bible to the young people.
- To help the young people apply this teaching to themselves.
- To demonstrate this application in their own lives.

Implications

To fulfil these responsibilities a children's and youth leader will:

- Read the Bible for themselves, pray and live out the Christian faith.
- Pray regularly for the young people in their group.
- Work as part of a team that meets regularly to plan the teaching programme.
- Be responsible to the team leader or appropriate church staff member.
- Expect to spend some time planning well for each teaching session.
- Aim to develop friendships with the young people through social activity.
- Consider training as an important priority.
- Be familiar with and agree to the church's Child Protection Policy.

The answer is a resounding 'yes!'. Although we shouldn't drag secular models into Christian ministry all over the place, we do need to know what good practice looks like. And we need to sensitively, but firmly, communicate that goal of good practice to our leaders. With God's help we will have humble, Bible-believing people at the heart of our teams. They will grow to understand what is required and be willing to be trained as necessary.

So, if the majority of this chapter looks like a pipe dream for your situation, let's conclude by drawing the starting line as opposed to the finishing line. You don't have to be a high-profile, large city church to reach it. All churches can reach the start line, even if they are small, rural and full of the generationally challenged. Even your church can.

The starting line is simply to have genuine Christians on your team. By that I mean people who recognise Jesus as Lord and Saviour and accept the authority of His Word, the Bible. The best we can do for our children and young people is to put them in the care of humble, honest and loving Christians.

Roger Fawcett is currently Youth Minister at St John's, Hartford, Cheshire. He has 15 years' experience working with young people. He is married to Fran and has three children. In the past, he has worked as a surf instructor, a grave digger and a sound studio technician. Jobs he would like to do in the future include being a blues musician, travel writing and driving a steam train.

CASE STUDY

Toni—Pathfinder leader (11-14s)

This age group is full of questions and won't be fobbed off with shallow answers. If you give them the opportunity to ask questions, they will—that's what I love about them. When I was a kid, I remember sitting in Sunday School classes where things never quite made sense. So I have made it my aim to give the Pathfinders the opportunity to see that the Bible *does* add up and that Christianity is worth it.

To do this I have discovered that there is no alternative to investing the time to make sure that I really understand what I'm teaching, so you can do it to the best of your ability. When I started, I realised that I had so much to learn, so I enrolled on a theological correspondence course.*

From the very beginning I wanted the young people to feel part of an extended family. I knew we had to earn the right to be heard and they needed to see us in action outside Sunday mornings. Particularly when we first took on the group, they watched everything about us closely, our reactions to our own children and so on.

We recently had a very successful 'Bring a friend' Sunday when several group members brought friends. The guests were under no illusions that Bible teaching was at the centre of what we do, so there was no need to make apologies. We let the Bible set the agenda and the questions and discussion flowed. It's also great to be part of a team with others who have the same knowledge of and desire for God's Word, so that we can encourage and sharpen each other as we teach.

* *The Moore College correspondence course is designed to help people develop their understanding of the Bible. More details from the appendix on page 156.*

Bible Study
Read 1 Thessalonians 2 v 1-12

1. Paul is countering criticism of his work with the Thessalonians (v 1-6). What does he say are his aims and motivation? Discuss what our motives must be. How can Paul's defence help us when our work with young people comes under attack?

2. How does Paul describe his relationship with the Christians in Thessalonica? (v 7, 8, 11) What are some of the other characteristics of this relationship? How can our gospel work benefit from a similar attitude? Discuss what makes gospel work with young people a delight.

3. What has Paul's behaviour been like as he witnessed to the Thessalonians? What clues are there that Paul's ministry was hard work? Discuss what keeps us going through difficult times when working with children and young people.

4. Pick out some of the verbs that Paul uses to describe his work in Thessalonica. How can they be applied to youth and children's work? Discuss what good practice in youthwork would look like from these verses.

3. The whole package

How can we teach the whole counsel of God?

THERE ARE A NUMBER of American TV drama series, like *Alias*, *24* and *The West Wing*, which are popular in the UK. The format of all of these dramas is pretty similar—they run for a season of twenty or so episodes and, although, to a certain extent, each episode stands alone, there is an underlying story, which runs through the whole season.

So while it is possible to watch and even enjoy the odd episode in isolation, the way to get the most out of the series is to watch them all in order, because then you get the whole story and the individual episodes make sense, in their context.

As an avid fan of these drama series, I've lost count of the number of times I've said to people who've watched one or two random episodes and not really liked them, "Unless you watch the whole series and get the big picture, you'll never really enjoy it, because you won't know what's going on."

Sometimes, exactly the same can be said in Christian children's and youth groups, because, very often, even in really good groups, we teach Bible stories as individual episodes without ever the teaching the whole Bible story.

As a result, even in churches where teaching the Bible is taken seriously, many young people in Sunday schools and youth groups grow up without any real understanding of the Bible's overall message. They may know Bible stories and, hopefully, will have gained useful biblical truth from those stories, but they may well have missed out on the big picture of God's unfolding revelation, plan and dealings with His people.

As young people get older, this teaching of Bible stories is often replaced (or supplemented) with teaching of key Bible doctrines—grace, forgiveness, judgment, substitution, incarnation etc. But once again, often these doctrines are taught in isolation and are not set in the backdrop of the big picture of God's revelation, plan and dealings with His people.

A great way of testing to see if young people have got a good understanding of the overall story of the Bible is to ask them to put the following people into the order that they appear in the Bible:

Daniel, Noah, Paul, Moses, Jesus, Abraham, Adam, Jacob, David.

Alternatively, you can try something similar with the following Bible events:

> Sin entering the world, the flood, the cross, slavery in Egypt, creation, David and Goliath, the return of Jesus, promises to Abraham, Daniel in the lions' den, crossing the Red Sea, the birth of Jesus, the resurrection, the conversion of Saul, the 10 Commandments and the fall of Jericho.

Although many young people in our groups will be able to identify most of these people and events, you may be surprised by how many struggle to put them into the right order.

The implications of NOT having a big picture understanding of God's revelation, plan and dealings with His people are enormous:

First—Bible study becomes boring and repetitive

There are, in fact, only so many Bible stories that you can teach. If you are only going to teach Bible stories, then there are great quantities of biblical material that don't fit neatly into a 'Bible story' category, including, for example, most of Old Testament law and prophesy and most New Testament letters.

Leaving out this much material gives a smaller 'resource' from which to chose stories, and inevitably means that young people who spend any time in Sunday School or youth groups will end up hearing the same stories over and over again. Although repeating stories aids learning, and it may be possible to develop stories in an age-appropriate way, there are limits to this.

Second—Application is weak

It's very hard to apply a Bible story or doctrine correctly and refreshingly, without setting it in its biblical context. The biblical context allows us to understand why the events described happened and were written about. It helps us to see for whom it was written; why it was written; what the original participants or readers were to make of it, etc.

This, in turn, makes it much easier as we try to understand what a particular passage, story or doctrine, has to say to us today. If we teach Bible stories or doctrines in isolation, then it is very difficult to make these same applications. More often than not, we end up teaching moralistic ('do as they did') applications, or we bolt on our own standard applications— read your Bible, say your prayers, be nice, tell other people about Jesus. This, too, becomes repetitive and boring.

Third—Assurance is undermined

Without a decent understanding of the big picture of God's revelation, plan and dealings with His people, it's hard to establish and be certain of our place in that plan.

For example, why do the promises that God made to Abraham way back in Genesis 12 have any implication or assurance for me today? Or why does God rescuing the Israelites from slavery in Egypt give me any assurance that He will rescue me?

Interestingly, when Paul wants to reassure the Ephesians that their faith is genuine and well-placed, he reminds them of the big picture of God's plan and their place in it (see Ephesians chapter 1).

Fourth—Lack of future perspective

Whenever you look at the big picture story of the Bible there is always a sense of looking forward. So from as early as Genesis 3, we are encouraged to look forward to the family line of promise from whom the 'serpent crusher' will come (Genesis 3 v 15), and from Genesis 12 onwards we are looking forward to the fulfilment of the promises to Abraham.

God's people in slavery look forward to rescue; in the desert they look forward to entering the promised land; and later on, in exile, they look forward to returning to the land.

The Old Testament prophets point us forward to God's perfect kingdom, ruled by God's perfect rescuer king. And, although in the New Testament we see the beginning of these promises being fulfilled, we are still pointed forward to the return of the Lord Jesus, when God's everlasting and perfect kingdom will be fully, finally and visibly established.

As Christians today, it is right that we look back to the history of God's dealings with His people and, supremely, to the life, death, resurrection and ascension of the Lord Jesus; but there ought also to be a future perspective to what we believe and how we live. Teaching Bible stories in isolation tends to encourage us to only look backwards without giving us that future perspective.

How to teach the big picture

Even if we can see that teaching the big picture of God's revelation, plan and dealings with His people is important, the question still remains: how do we do that?

Knowing the big picture for ourselves

The first step in teaching the overall story of the Bible is to make sure that we understand and have a decent grasp of the big picture ourselves.

One way of starting to think about our own understanding of the big story of the Bible is to ask ourselves this question: 'If you could sum up the whole message of the Bible in a sentence or a paragraph, how would you do it?' Or 'What are the key truths, doctrines, phrases or words that we would expect to find in a summary of the Bible's whole message?'

Also, it's well worth reading one of the books currently available which present an overview of the Bible's story. These include *Gospel and Kingdom* by Graham Goldsworthy and *God's Big Picture* by Vaughan Roberts*.

Both these books take the theme of the kingdom of God as they explain the big story of the Bible. Goldsworthy describes the kingdom of God as God's people in God's place under God's rule, and then works through the story of the Bible to show how this kingdom comes about. This provides a useful framework for working out where individual Bible stories fit into the big picture of God's unfolding revelation, plan and dealings with His people.

Goldsworthy summarises his Bible overview in the diagram opposite:

---

* See appendix on page 156 for further details.

	GOD'S PEOPLE	GOD'S PLACE	GOD'S RULE
EDEN	ADAM & EVE	THE GARDEN	GOD'S WORD
ISRAEL	ABRAHAM	CANAAN	COVENANT
	ISRAEL UNDER MOSES	PROMISED LAND	SINAI COVENANT
	ISRAEL UNDER MONARCHY	LAND, JERUSALEM, TEMPLE	SINAI COVENANT
PROPHECY	FAITHFUL REMNANT OF ISRAEL	RESTORED LAND, JERUSALEM, TEMPLE	NEW COVENANT WRITTEN ON THE HEART

JESUS CHRIST

NEW TESTAMENT	NEW ISRAEL —THOSE 'IN CHRIST'	NEW TEMPLE —WHERE CHRIST DWELLS	NEW COVENANT —CHRIST'S RULE

Diagram taken from *Gospel and Kingdom* by Graeme Goldsworthy.
Used by permission. See appendix on page 156 for details.

Teaching an Overview

When it comes to teaching an overview of the Bible, there are, generally speaking, two approaches that one can take:

The first is to teach an 'Historical Timeline' overview, which works through the key events in the order in which they happen. This is the approach taken with *The King, the snake and the promise* material for younger children and also with the *Out of this World* material in the *Lightening Bolt* series for 11-14 year olds.*

The strong point in both of these packages is that during the series, group members create a timeline of the Bible's overall story. It is really useful to keep this timeline displayed so that future Bible stories and teaching can be easily set into their historical biblical context. Although *The King, the snake and the promise* is aimed at younger children, it is possible to adapt it for an older group.

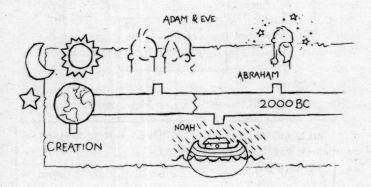

The second approach is to teach a Bible overview by teaching the big themes of the Bible: kingdom, rescue, revelation, love etc.

---

* Full details of these resources are in the appendix on page 156.

CASE STUDY

Alison Mitchell

Children are often very familiar with well-known Bible stories, but have no idea how those stories fit together. Teaching them the big picture of Bible history helps them to see where everything fits in. It also reinforces the fact that the Bible events are part of history, and that they happened to real people living in real places.

A Bible overview is a fantastic way to help children discover what God is like. For example, the Old Testament shows us again and again that God's people are faithless, but that God Himself is always faithful and can be trusted.

I remember teaching the events of Exodus, looking at the way God kept His promise to rescue His people. He sent the ten plagues, brought His people safely out of Egypt, and then delivered them from the Egyptian army. Later, when the Israelites were ready to enter the promised land, Moses sent twelve spies to check it out first. The spies came back with reports of a fantastic land, but with some worryingly big people living in it! The Israelites had to choose whether or not they would trust God to bring them into the land He had promised, and defeat those huge people.

I asked the children to vote on it. Would the Israelites trust God to help them? Or would they be too scared to go into the land? Almost every child thought the Israelites would trust God. Why? Because God had already done such amazing miracles to bring them out of Egypt.

When I told the children that the Israelites *hadn't* trusted God, they were shocked. One boy's mouth actually fell open in amazement! The children had seen the bigger picture— they knew that God was looking after His people in a wonderful way—and they were astounded that the Israelites didn't trust Him. It gave a fantastic opportunity to talk about God's character, and why *we* can totally trust Him, too.

This is more like the approach that Goldsworthy and Roberts use in their books and is used in the 'teachinglittleones.com' teaching material.

Whichever way we decide to teach an overview, we're likely to face a couple of problems or issues:

Teaching difficult parts of the Bible

An area of concern for people involved in teaching the Bible to young people is often the question of whether and how to teach difficult parts of the Bible. In any serious attempt to teach an overview of the Bible, there are going to be some sections that are more palatable than others.

For instance, is it right to teach young people about God's judgment or to teach the sections of the Bible where we see God's judgment demonstrated? What about the parts where people do terrible things in the Bible, or even where God appears to encourage people to do terrible things—like Abraham being told to sacrifice Isaac or the occupiers of the promised land being ordered to spare no one?

The answer is that *we can and must* teach these parts of the Bible, but we need to do it in a way that is sensitive, clear and appropriate for the age-group that we are teaching. These stories and episodes are part of the rich canvas of the Bible and help us to understand God and His dealings with His people.

Teaching appropriately may mean emphasising the truth contained in a story, without dwelling on the details of the episode. Interestingly, a good understanding of the Bible's big story will help to put these, sometimes unsavoury, stories into their biblical context, which helps, in turn, to make them more understandable.

For instance, when we know that God has promised to make Abraham into the father of all of God's people and that, despite Abraham's regular failures, God has been training him to be the man that He wants him to be, we begin to understand why God tests Abraham by asking him to sacrifice Isaac and why Abraham is willing to do so.

In fact, what looks like a terrible story is actually a fantastic moment in the history of God's dealings with His people because Abraham—the father of God's people—finally demonstrates that he is properly trusting in God.

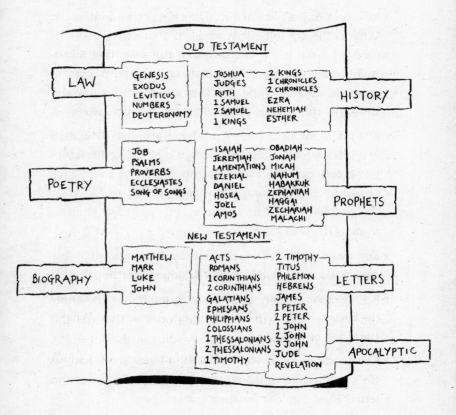

Teaching different types of biblical literature

It may seem very obvious to say it, but not all biblical literature is the same, which means that not all biblical literature can be taught and applied in the same way.

The Bible is made up of historical narrative (eg: Exodus), prophetic literature (eg: Isaiah), poetry (eg: Psalms), biography (eg: Mark), letters (eg: Romans) and apocalyptic writing (eg: Revelation).

Each of these different literary genres need to be handled differently.

- Key questions to ask when studying **historical narrative** are: What is the big thing that we learn about God from this passage? What would the people at the time have understood from these events? To what extent are we to copy or avoid the actions of the people described in this passage? How does this passage point us towards the Lord Jesus?

- Key questions to ask when studying **prophetic literature** are: What were the circumstances of the original hearers of this prophecy? How would the prophecy have warned the unfaithful and encouraged the faithful? Where do we see this prophecy fulfilled? How does this prophecy point us towards the Lord Jesus?

- Key question to ask when studying **biography** is: What does this passage tell us about the person it is describing?

- Key questions to ask when studying **poetry** are: What are the circumstances in which the poem was written? What is the mood of the poem?

- Key questions to ask when studying a **letter** are: What was the circumstance of the writer and original hearers of this letter? How does our situation compare?

- Key question to ask when approaching **apocalyptic writing** is: Is this imagery used elsewhere in the Bible?

For a fuller explanation and discussion of these issues see the appendix on page 156 for suggested books.

Conclusion

Although there is plenty more which could be said on the subject of teaching the whole counsel of God, I hope that it is clear from this short chapter that it is very important that we teach the big story of the Bible, so that young people grow up with a full understanding of God, His plan and their place in it.

Nick Margesson is a full-time youth worker at St. Helen's, Bishopsgate. He is married to Ellie, and they have two children. Nick chairs *Capital Youthworks*, an interdenominational charity for young people and youth leaders. That means Nick helps to sort out SORTED, an annual day of Bible teaching for teenagers.

Bible Study

Stephen was one of the leaders of the early church. After being falsely accused of speaking against God, he was dragged in front of the Sanhedrin, the Jewish council, to defend himself. Stephen's speech to the Sanhedrin was a summary of Bible history...

Read Acts 7 v 1-60

1. Make a list of the key Bible characters Stephen mentions in his speech.

2. Which character does Stephen give the most detail about? Why do you think he did this?

3. What does this passage tell us about God's character and His dealings with His people?

4. In v51-53 Stephen applies Old Testament history to his New Testament audience. What application does he make? Can you make this same application to the children or young people in your group? Why / why not?

Stephen used a Bible overview to rebuke and challenge his hearers. In Psalm 105, an overview of Bible history is used in a very different way—to encourage God's people to praise their great, promise-keeping God.

Use the words of **Psalm 105 v 1-4** to praise and thank God now.

4. The Word on the street

How can we encourage children and young people to read the Bible?

OVERHEARING CHILDREN OR YOUNG PEOPLE talking about the Bible is one of those rare treats that can knock you for six— the great realisation that they're reading it for themselves, plundering God's Word, and it's having an impact on their lives and their friends' lives. We spend so much of our time teaching and talking about the Bible with them, yet we're surprised when they take it in and start delving into it by themselves. We sometimes forget the power of God's awesome Word, and the work of the Holy Spirit in opening up the Bible to them.

Perhaps we're even guilty of not expecting them to read the Bible for themselves at all. There can be the assumption that young people hardly read books anymore, so they're not going to open up a dusty old Bible. And because we don't expect them to get stuck into the Bible, we don't encourage it as much as we could. Let's not sell God's Word short.

If your heart's desire is to bring children and young people to know Christ and to live for Him, then employ the best home tutor you have available—the Bible itself. Strive to get them into the habit of reading the Bible for themselves—it's the best teacher they'll ever encounter.

Need any further reasons? Well, it pleases God, as they get to grips with the word of truth (2 Timothy 2 v 15); they need it for growth, just as a baby craves its mother's milk (1 Peter 2 v 2); it aids their discernment of spiritual truth (Acts 17 v 11); and will build their knowledge and understanding (Psalm 119 v 130); so they can share their faith more effectively (1 Peter 3 v 15); and it helps them to fight against sin (Psalm 119 v 11).

First things first

If you're anything like me, one of the things that limits the enthusiasm you put into encouraging regular Bible reading is the state of your own Bible reading efforts. It's something we all struggle with at some point, and usually ends up with us wallowing in guilty feelings rather than coming up with a new strategy.

Just do it—as Nike's adverts annoyingly told us a while back. Set yourself a time which you can fully commit to reading your Bible and praying most days. Make sure you have daily Bible notes or a reading plan—it's much easier to jump into it every day, if you've got a plan laid out, and notes to guide you through the Bible and challenge you. And if you miss a few days, or even a few weeks, don't wallow! Pick up where you left off, and get stuck in again. If your last Bible notes or reading plan weren't your cup of tea, try something else.

Once you start reaping the benefits of regularly reading the Bible, it's so much easier to encourage children and young people to do the same.

Create a culture

Now you can start creating a culture of Bible reading within your Sunday School class, kid's club or youth group. Encourage them to bring Bibles along to meetings, so that they expect to be reading the Bible. Show them that reading God's Word is normal and natural for young Christians. If any of them don't have Bibles, give them one!

It's obvious, I know, but we can be guilty of expecting unchurched kids to fit straight into our churchy ways, without meeting them half way. So you might want to give them a crash course on the Bible; what it is, who wrote it, what's in it, how to find different books, the big picture etc. You could do a short Bible overview spanning a few weeks. And when you mention Bible passages or verses, get them to turn to them (and read them out loud), so they get used to handling the Bible and reading it for themselves.

Take the alien-ness out of the Bible, so that it becomes a normal practice to turn to God's Word, not a last resort. And make it fun. With younger children (and maybe older ones too), you could use a game or 'Bible-drill' every time they turn to a passage.

A daily habit

The simplest way to encourage regular Bible reading is to promote daily Bible reading notes. Do some reconnaissance work to find Bible notes that are suitable for the age range in your group. Most important is finding notes that teach the Bible faithfully, that encourage the reader to interact with God's Word and apply it to their lives. That's much more important than finding ones that look the part.

If you've got the funds, buy everyone in your group an issue to get them started. If you haven't got the cash, maybe a few people in your church will sponsor subscriptions. It's a good way for older church members to get involved with children and young people in your church, and it provides a link between them. Maybe they'll even ask them how they're getting along with the notes (there's nothing wrong with a little friendly pressure).

The reason why Bible reading notes are so good is that they encourage children and young people to read the Bible regularly. Hopefully, the notes will also take them through different books of the Bible, explaining the tough parts along the way, and highlighting the specific relevance of God's Word to their lives. Remember there are horses for courses, so not everyone will take to the notes you choose, and you might have to try a different approach with them. And even if they're using Bible notes that aren't great, at least they're reading the Bible for themselves, and that's the main objective.

Try to emphasise that they needn't worry if they miss a few days or weeks. They can pick it up and start again. It doesn't matter whether or not they're reading the notes allocated for that specific day, as long as they are reading the Bible. And if those notes aren't working for them, maybe it's time to try something else.

If a number of children/young people in your group are regularly reading their Bibles, get them to feed back what they've read or learned that week. Perhaps you could prime someone different every week to report on what they've been reading, and to share some of what God has taught them. This will encourage them to read the Bible and hopefully will encourage others in the group to give it a go too. It might even spark off discussions and questions about specific passages or certain teaching in the Bible.

Enthusiasm breeds interest. In a kid's club I help with, I was chuffed to hear several eight year old boys arguing over the specific words of their memory verses, and trying to get their heads around what it actually meant.

A weekly habit

Since enthusiasm breeds interest, get your group to encourage each other to get plugged into studying the Bible. If some of them are particularly keen on it, set up small groups where they meet together regularly, with the specific aim of studying the Bible and praying together. It could take the form of an optional Bible-study meeting for the keenies, or something more informal between just three or four of the group.

You may think it's appropriate for an adult to lead this group or you may want to leave them to it. The former option allows you to shape a Bible-study programme for their needs, whereas the latter encourages them to discover Bible truths more for themselves, without being spoon-fed. It also provides them with an environment where they can honestly share their thoughts, worries, problems and prayer requests with each other, without the embarrassment of having a leader around. This way they start to become accountable to each other, plus there's an element of excitement if they're starting up something of their own without adult intervention.

For younger children, new Christians, or those asking questions about Christianity, a one-to-one approach could prove more appropriate. Suggest meeting up with them once a week to study the Bible together and pray. This allows you to give the child/young person the spiritual food they specifically need.

For example, if they're not yet a Christian, you could work your way through Mark's gospel, or perhaps a short evangelistic course (there are several good ones around at the moment). If it's a new Christian you're meeting with, perhaps Colossians or 1 Peter would be a good starting point. Find out if the person you're meeting with has any particular issues they want to deal with.

If you do meet up for one-to-one Bible study, try not to be too heavy-handed. Make sure they are comfortable. This might involve showing them how to actually find different parts of the Bible. Or it might mean a few ice-breaking questions before you start. Try to get them to do most of the hard work, so that they discover what the Bible is teaching. Don't just tell them, but let them work it out for themselves, so that they are truly interacting with God's Word. Then stand back and watch God speaking directly to them.

Be a bombardier

On Fridays, a group of guys from our office play football at lunchtime. We play against a team of much younger and fitter students. They often outplay us, making us look stupid at times with their great passing and little tricks. But they don't get many shots in, so they rarely score many goals. However, us old duffers play with far less finesse, yet rain shots in on their goal. Eventually, some of them go in and we even manage to beat them sometimes!

Bombarding their goal with shots from various angles pays off. And that can be a useful tactic when trying to encourage children and young people to read their Bibles. Try lots of different things. Bombard them with different ideas to help them get stuck into God's Word.

> All Scripture is God-breathed and is useful for teaching, rebuking, correcting and training in righteousness, so that the man of God may be thoroughly equipped for every good work.
> 2 Timothy 3 v 16-17

This is God's Word we're talking about here! As children's workers and youth workers we're passionate about helping young people to grow in their faith and become disciples of Jesus. The Bible must be entirely central to any discipleship. We want to see children and young people training in righteousness, so that they're fully equipped to serve God. For that training, they need to be studying, learning from and memorising God's Word. So we need to try every method at our disposal to encourage them to do that. Be a bombardier. Carpet bomb them with the Bible!

Ideas for bombardiers:

Here are a few more ideas for you to consider (or sneer at and then throw in the bin):

- Give out free Bible notes to get them started. That could mean buying them all daily Bible notes or producing your own Bible-reading programme to hand out.

- Try to build into your meetings/clubs a time for the group to discuss or share something from what they've been reading.

- Encourage them to ask questions about stuff they don't fully understand. You could have a regular *Question Time* slot. Not only will this help the children/young people in

CASE STUDY

Jim Overton

Jim is Director of Cambridge & District Youth for Christ. 'The main thing I would say, if it's not stating the obvious, is not to be scared of the big book. I remember doing 'Just Looking' groups on several occasions following mission events, and having to use the Bible with young people who didn't know which way up to hold it. At the end of the day, I think the more you can actually get young people to hold a Bible with you in the room, actually open it, and actually read it to find the information in it, the better.

'The number of young people who will look into the sky, straining for an answer in a Bible study, is incredible! The more they engage with the actual text of the Bible in groups, the less intimidated they will be by the thought of tackling it in private.

'The other thing to say is that we get much more serious with the Bible when we need answers. Young people love the stuff in the front of the *Gideon Bible* that tells them where to find help on specific issues. It's not a strictly thorough approach, but it does get them started. Sometimes as leaders we can do a Bible study to teach them, and when they come to us with questions we give them the benefit of our wisdom. But *showing them* where the answers are in the Bible is so much more helpful—as well as keeping us bound by the truth, it equips them to know where to go for future answers.

'We learn so much more when we are preparing to teach others than we do when just soaking up a sermon. So, if that works for us, why not with young people? I invite them to share a 'thought for the day' which can be anything from the Bible at all. Even the shy and retiring come up with something and it's usually pretty good. It helps them no end.'

their understanding of the Word, but it will also keep you on your toes and help you to get your own Bible knowledge and doctrine sorted.

- Memory verses (don't groan!). Yes, it's old-fashioned, and, if you're like me, it could well give you nightmares from your youth. But learning memory verses is such a practical, tangible way of getting God's Word into your mind and writing it on your heart. Of course, you'll have to learn them yourself too...

- For younger children: handouts! Give them sheets to take home and bring back, so you're encouraging them to delve into the Bible when they're away from church/club. They're time-consuming to create but well worth it. Sheets that encourage children to look up Bible passages, with puzzles that relate to what they're reading, go down particularly well in my experience. You could set up a star chart with stars awarded for completed sheets and memory verses remembered.

Non–readers

What about children or young people who can't or don't read so much? For lots of young people, reading isn't a big part of their culture, it's not something they do regularly. It can seem much more of a chore than a pleasure. This makes it hard to promote Bible reading to them.

If they hardly read anything at all, why would they bother with the Bible? You have to get creative. Give them smaller chunks of the Bible to read, in a easy-to-read version. You might want to give them a graphic novel (comic book) version of the Bible, or Bible stories. Okay, it's not perfect, but if they're not reading the Bible at all, it's a start. You could encourage them to listen to the Bible on CD or to look up websites that look at God's Word. It can be hard work getting some people to open their Bibles at all, but we've got to try every route possible to get them learning from God's Word.

Let's make the Bible the focus of our times together. Let's make it natural and expected for us to open God's Word together, and share from it and question it. Let's get young people reading the Bible for themselves. Let's watch God transforming them with His Word.

Martin Cole writes Discover daily Bible notes for 11s-13s and is involved in children's work at Hillside Church, Wimbledon. Martin foolishly supports Chesterfield FC and passionately hates bananas.

Bible Study
Read Psalm 119 v 9–16

1. What was the writer's attitude towards God's Word?

2. According to the writer, how can God's Word help the spiritual growth of young people?

3. What can *you* do to meditate more on God's Word and consider His ways (v 15)?

4. What practical steps can you take to help your group hide God's Word in their hearts (v 11)?

5. Make a list of Bible verses/passages that have been helpful to you, and that you think would be great for your group to memorise.

5. Mix and match

How do we pitch our teaching for a mixed group of churched and unchurched children and young people?

IN MANY CHURCHES today, the answer to this problem has been to have completely separate groups, which never meet with each other, and which tackle different objectives:

- The 'detached work' is aimed at the 'un-churched', to make contact with them, befriend them and hopefully earn the right to share the gospel with them. It is often cutting-edge, fun, and although the Bible is important, it's not generally at the centre of the work.

- The 'Young People's Fellowship' is aimed at the 'churched' young people, to nurture and disciple them, teach them and help them to see how they are expected to live as Christians today. Generally, it is less exciting and fun, but does have a lot more teaching at the centre of the work.

Although these scenarios are broad generalisations, they represent much of what happens in children's and youth work around the UK today. There are, however, good reasons for considering bringing these two groups together. Our aim is to make disciples of Jesus—disciples who will live for Jesus in a hostile world, and who will be equipped to reach out to others with the message of salvation. In the 'two groups model' you effectively have a cosy club for Christians, and a group of pagans being evangelised by adults. Neither of these achieves the bigger objective.

The churched children get used to having their own nice, safe environment—no training for being in the world. Nor do they have the opportunity for 'live' evangelism. But worse than that, we are actually short-changing the unchurched! If the gospel is

---

DEFINITIONS:

'**Churched**': children and/or young people who are regular within the group and have been for more than a term. 'Churched' does not mean 'Christian', although some may well be Christians. 'Churched' refers to them being regular in attendance and becoming acclimatised to what happens in and around the group and church.

Un-churched': children and/or young people who are new to the group and unfamiliar with the way that the group operates. They will also, almost certainly, be unfamiliar with the Bible, Christianity and church. Through regular attendance they will become 'churched' members, but this does not make them Christian.

---

both taught and caught, it makes sense that the best context for hearing the gospel has to be in a group where they can see and spend time with people of their own age who are living the Christian life. Our challenge, and the big question before us, is... can both objectives—evangelism and discipleship—be achieved in one group, especially when it comes to pitching the teaching?

As I considered this question, and looked back on many years of working with children and young people in different settings and from different backgrounds, many of my memories were of the difficulties and failures of trying to achieve this joint aim, in one group. However, as I thought it through in more detail, I was reminded of many successes too, and I hope to share and build on some of these.

Let me start by saying that there is no quick and easy formula, which, when applied, turns your children's and youth work into the thriving, successful and 'bursting at the seams' group we all want—producing new converts and developing focused and very committed children and young people, who are dying to get out to change the world for Jesus.

What is required from leaders is a passion for God's Word, commitment, focus, perseverance, prayer, support, a heart for children and young people, hard work and dependence on God's grace through His Spirit. We have the privilege of being used by God in His work. We must never forget that, and need to ensure that we have prayer and the study of God's Word at the heart of our own personal life.

To this end, the most important tool we have in children's and youth work is God's Word. Before we even think about systems, programmes, aims and objectives, we must have established a personal discipline of reading Scripture, be growing in our knowledge and understanding of it, have a commitment to studying and wrestling with it, and be able to pass on a passion for it, especially to those in our care.

As we study the Bible, we need to apply questions like the ones below, to help ensure we don't get the wrong meaning. We too easily make a passage of Scripture mean what *we* want it to, instead of what *God* intended it to mean.

When studying, always concentrate on the text and only move to how you will teach it when you are satisfied that you understand the main points of the passage.

Helpful questions to ask:

- What does the passage say?
- Why does it say it?
- Why does it say it in this way?
- What is the main point?
- How does it apply?

(If you would like further help in how to understand a Bible passage, see the suggested books in the appendix on page 156.)

Teaching: the example of Jesus

Jesus is our best example. He knew the Scriptures. **Read Matthew 4 v 1-11** and **Luke 24 v 13-35** (esp. v 25-27, 32).

So how did Jesus, during His ministry, tackle the challenge of teaching people who were at different stages of a relationship with Him? Some committed to Him... some sceptical... some wondering who He was... and some aggressive towards Him.

Jesus taught in three ways:

1. The crowd in the hearing of the disciples
2. The disciples in the hearing of the crowd
3. The disciples alone

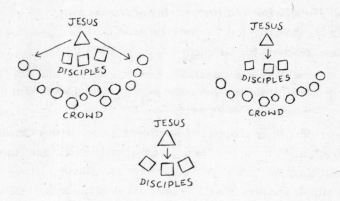

1. The crowd in the hearing of the disciples:

In Mark 4 v 1-9 we read Jesus' parable of the sower. Verse 1 sets the scene:

> The crowd that gathered round him was so large that he got into a boat and sat in it out on the lake, while all the people were along the shore at the water's edge. **Mark 4 v 1b**

Verse 2 explains what Jesus did: 'He taught them many things by parables'. However, verse 9 finishes with, 'He who has ears to hear, let him hear'.

Jesus has finished with the crowd. He is cryptic in warning them that what He has said requires thought and action in response, but He doesn't explain what He has said... well, not to the crowd anyway.

This is not the only example of Jesus using parables with the crowds and not explaining what He had been saying. He has left it in the air... Why?

- Should we sometimes teach by telling stories and not necessarily explaining what they mean?

2. The disciples in the hearing of the crowd:

In Matthew chapters 5-7, the Sermon on the Mount, we read of Jesus teaching His disciples:

> Now when He saw the crowds, He went up on a mountainside and sat down. His disciples came to Him, and He began to teach them, saying... **Matthew 5 v 1-2**

The next three chapters of Matthew's gospel cover extensive teaching to those who were followers of Jesus. He gave them teaching, instructions and commands about living, setting an example and how to treat others—and all of this in the hearing of those who weren't followers at this time. Jesus' teaching alone would have been useful to the crowd listening—but they would also, in time, have benefited from seeing the results of that teaching in the changed lives of the disciples.

Read Matthew 7 v 28-29

How did the crowd react to this teaching?

- Is this an example of how you teach, with a focus on discipleship?

- How do we teach and encourage those who haven't made a commitment?

- Does this assume a certain level of understanding of the Bible already?

3. The disciples alone:

Returning to the passage in Mark, we have a chance to look in on Jesus teaching His disciples alone.

Read Mark 4 v 10-20.

Once Jesus was alone, what did the disciples do? Why do you think they came to Him?

There is no doubt in my own mind that the disciples' relationship with Jesus was such that they were desperate to understand as much as they could from Him. Having heard the parable, they didn't know what it meant and wanted to know what Jesus was saying. He had withdrawn, and so in privacy they were able to approach Him and ask the questions which would unlock the meaning for them.

- Is this perhaps too exclusive?

- Can we set up a group separate from any more inclusive work, just to help those who are already Christians or have a desire to know more?

How does Jesus' teaching example help us?

First of all, let us define our existing membership. Let's define the crowd as those who are 'un-churched' children and young people in our group; and let's define the disciples as those who are 'churched' children and young people.

In terms of a mixed group, both 'churched' and 'un-churched', we must first consider, very carefully, who we are aiming at, principally, in our teaching and what we are trying to achieve through it.

Do we, generally, teach discipleship issues, aimed principally at the 'churched', but with the 'un-churched' listening in, with the aim of teaching and encouraging the children and young people to live out their relationship with Jesus? Or do we, generally, teach evangelistically, looking to reach the 'un-churched' and teach and encourage them to commit to following Jesus?

In reality, our aim should be to teach a mixture of both—but I put 'generally' above, because there needs to be a clear direction for the majority of the teaching: discipleship or evangelistic.

For a church and Bible-based group, I think discipleship should be the foundational objective, but with regular opportunities to be evangelistic, through the teaching syllabus and by presenting special evangelistic events.

The implications:

To meet this challenge, we must ensure that we address the following points in our teaching:

- **Engage the 'un-churched':** get them interested and understanding, while not boring the 'churched' and not diluting God's Word;

- **Use inclusive language:** not using jargon and church speak, but also not losing the meaning of key and foundational words which explain faith and God's plan;

- **Work at unity:** ensuring the group is not divided and ends up as two separate groups—'inside kids' and 'outside kids' / 'churched' and 'un-churched';

- **Don't just teach thematically:** follow through Bible books and ensure the whole counsel of Scripture is covered over time. Maintain a balanced teaching programme;

- **Preparation:** there are no short cuts to success. Time spent in understanding the Bible, and working at communicating it well, is essential. 'Ready to use' and 'off the shelf' teaching resources may not be effective, especially for you personally. They can encourage bad habits, particularly in preparation. You need to put the work in and will gain from a greater confidence and understanding if you do. Our number one resource is the Bible;

- **Nurture a passion for God's Word:** devote yourself to understanding it and passing on that passion to others, especially children and young people. Be passionate when you talk about the Bible. Model the excitement that God's Word gives.

Although there will always be new ways of reaching and communicating with children and young people, 'churched' and 'un-churched', God's Word never changes and will always be the one non-negotiable in our package. It is sad when, as leaders, we spend so much time putting together attractive programmes, or making extravagant or clever presentations, but very little on actually teaching the Bible. That's the challenge for all of us... making God's Word accessible and understandable.

Summary

In summary, I would want to emphasise these foundational principles:

- **Be Bible-centred:** remember that Scripture is, 'the power of God for the salvation of everyone who believes' (Romans 1 v 16);

- **Know your primary aim:** but don't lose sight of any secondary aims (discipleship/evangelism or evangelism/discipleship, plus establishing into the church fellowship);

- **Be prepared:** spend sufficient time studying and preparing God's Word before even considering how to teach it;

- **Know your group:** understand them well enough to be able to teach relevantly;

- **Communicate clearly:** ensure that God's Word is driving your communication—not the latest presentation gimmicks and ideas;

- **Pray:** ensure that God is in everything you do.

Our priority is, and should be, faithfulness in teaching God's Word, relevantly and appropriately, to all the children and young people, 'churched' and/or 'un-churched', in our groups.

Mark Tomlinson is over 40 and has been involved in children's and youth work for more than 28 years, the last 15 full-time. He will do ALMOST anything for the sake of the gospel. He has four children, Chris, Laura, David and Jamie, and lives in Cheadle. Being close to the centre of Manchester, they ALL support the real Manchester team... CITY!

CASE STUDY

The NET at St. Mary's Church, Cheadle

The NET (15's +) has been in existence, in one form or another, for more than 30 years, with the objective of building relationships with local young people, evangelising and discipling them, and ultimately helping them to integrate into the church fellowship. I'm sure there have been many successes and a few failures or at least challenges. However, in the last couple of years in particular, there have been some big encouragements, built on years of commitment, faithfulness, perseverance, hard work and above all God's grace.

The present numerical and spiritual growth has come through the work of the young people themselves, who have invited their friends to what is going on—but that doesn't happen unless they are confident in the structure and content of the group. This confidence has been nurtured because of the hard work of the leadership team.

The Structure:

Sundays: The group meets on a Sunday evening, on church premises, after the evening service. This is an opportunity for them to meet socially for chat, volleyball (or similar), chill time and some spiritual input, usually tackling the issues of the day from God's perspective. These are led either by NET leaders or special guests, with time for discussion and questions. The environment and atmosphere is friendly and warm, and the spiritual input is Bible-based, relevant to them, deep and challenging, but not overly long. It is a non-threatening environment, but with a clear message that the group is spiritual in focus. Those attending come from vastly different backgrounds and would be considered both 'churched' and 'un-churched', many with no prior church involvement.

Tuesdays: The group also meets on a Tuesday evening, in a leader's home, for Bible study, which many outside observers would deem 'boring with no frills'! However, the reality is far from it. Almost all those attending on a Sunday also attend the Tuesday, which begins with a social time of catching up over refreshments and generally having a laugh. The atmosphere is friendly, warm and, at times, raucous. When it is time for the study, the group divides up, usually into two groups, but depending on the choices, this could be more. Initially, a while ago, the two groups covered either 'the Youth Alpha Course (the basics of Christianity)' or a discipleship issue—for those who have been Christians for a while. More recently the two options have covered a look at the subject of angels, and the book of Revelation.

The success of the group has been the ease with which 'churched' and 'un-churched' young people have come together and been taught, without pressure, without feeling uncomfortable, or being expected to act in a particular way. Issues, and there have been many, are tackled sensitively, prayerfully and lovingly.

6. Letting the lion loose

How do we put a programme together?

THE GREAT PREACHER C.H. SPURGEON is quoted as saying that *'Scripture is like a lion. Whoever heard of defending a lion? Just turn it loose; it will defend itself.'* Our responsibility as youth and children's workers is to provide a structure where God's Word—'the lion'—can be let loose. Too often we spend most of our time seeking either to defend the lion, or never letting him out to do his work.

Hopefully, this short chapter will give a few pointers to help us create an environment where God's Word is let loose to save souls and mould disciples who love Christ.

Programme structure

The structure I'm going to suggest is one I've developed over many years as a youth worker. It involves two weekly meetings. The aim of the first meeting is primarily discipleship—as will be explained in the first half of this chapter. The aim of the second meeting is primarily evangelism.

In my experience, the discipleship meeting will probably happen on a Sunday or mid-week in small groups, and the evangelism meeting on a Friday or Saturday. But it doesn't really matter when, because the key thing is to be reaching both of these crucial needs:

- **Discipleship**—an environment where disciples are trained and taught the whole will of God.

- **Evangelism**—an environment where the young people can bring their friends to hear the gospel clearly presented.

Training disciples:

1. The living Word of God

The very first thing we need to be sure of when approaching the subject of teaching young people the Bible is that the Bible is the living Word of God. However gifted the youth or children's worker may be, none of us make the Bible come alive. Instead, it is the Bible that makes us come alive.

2. Clean hands

As the apostle Paul left the church at Ephesus, he claimed that he was innocent of their blood, because he had faithfully proclaimed to them the whole will of God (Acts 20 v 26–27). As youth and children's workers, this must be our ultimate aim, to bring glory to God by teaching His wonderful character to young people. The question is, where do we start?

Jesus regularly called His disciples away from the world, to privately teach them about the will of God and its transformation of their lives (Mark 3 v 7; 4 v 34; 7 v 17; 8 v 27; 9 v 28-31; 10 v 10, 23; 11 v 14; 12 v 43.). Jesus did this so that they would be strong enough to live holy lives in the world, bringing glory to God by winning the lost.

Therefore, our first aim must be to create a safe environment, where disciples are trained and taught the whole will of God. In the age that we're living in, giving young people the big picture of God's salvation plan is crucial.

3. Teaching the whole will of God

a. God's truth is important

In the post-Christian culture that we live in, the idea that history has meaning and is going somewhere is more and more alien and unpopular. The results of this are beginning to take root in the lives of young people and affect the culture that we live in. The past is either ignored as irrelevant, or for us to interpret in whatever way we decide.

Therefore, with no one to authoritatively interpret the past, the present lies open to the latest fashionable idea that people want to shout about. Everything is up for grabs, whether it concerns truth, morality or God. Any thoughts about the future are in a complete fog of confusion, leaving people with only one real choice—to live for the moment and for the best feeling they can obtain from the latest pleasure on offer.

Because of the present condition of our culture, it is crucial for our young people to get a good grasp of God's plan for His world, and its meaning and purpose as determined by Him. Our responsibility, as children's and youth leaders is to teach

God's truth accurately, digging into God's Word to reveal His plans and purposes. To reveal His truth in history, applied to our present, with an awesome impact on our future.

The way to do this is to ask the right questions of the Bible, such as:

1. What is the main point of this passage?
2. How does it fit into the passages before and after it?
3. How does it fit into the book that it is in?
4. How does the truth of the story fit into God's plan of salvation?
5. What is this passage teaching me about God?
6. What is this passage teaching me about mankind?
7. How is this truth going to change my life?

If we seek to answer these questions in our own preparation, then we can be sure that the young people will not only get an accurate Bible talk, but one that comes from a person who, like them, is being discipled by the Saviour.

b. God is King of history

The fact that God is the King of history is found on every page of the Bible. If we fail to let this lion of truth free to roam and dominate our thinking, then we can be sure that our children and young people's spiritual growth will be stunted. If our children and young people are to survive and remain holy in a godless world, then they have to be convinced that God is the sovereign ruler of it. As we seek to teach our young people the whole counsel of God, this truth will surround them with the confidence that is essential.

Here is a talk outline and discussion group questions that proclaim the wonderful truth of God's kingly rule:

TALK OUTLINE FOR PSALM 2

Aim

1. To reveal mankind's attitude towards God
   —Psalm 2 v 1-3.

2. To show that God responds in three ways to mankind's rebellion, all centred around God's King, Jesus—v 6.

3. The first two responses concern His laughter (v 4) and His anger (v 5, 9b).

4. The third response of God is His mercy—v 10-12. We therefore have a choice—to stand before the laughter and anger of God, or to kiss the Son and embrace His mercy.

Talk Headings

1. Your anger at God—v 1-3.

2. God's anger at you—v 4-5, 8-9, 12.

3. God's mercy to you—v 6, 10-12.

Discussion Group Questions

1. How does God describe people's attitude towards Jesus?

2. How have you seen, heard or experienced that?

3. How does God respond to people's attitude towards Jesus?

4. If you are a Christian, how does God's rule of His world give you confidence?

5. If you are not a Christian, what is your only hope?

c. Teaching the whole will of God reveals His character

When teaching God's plan of salvation, again and again His character blazes through as He reveals Himself by His acts and His words. For example, God's power is seen in creation, and His justice, faithfulness, patience and final judgment are all revealed in His covenants with Israel and how *they* chose to respond to them. In the Bible accounts of the life of Christ, we see exactly how He fulfilled God's plan of salvation.

In every area where Israel proved faithless, Jesus proves faithful (Luke 4 v 1-13). He lived a life perfectly pleasing to His Father, which finally lead to His death upon the cross. The life of Jesus should be the major motivation for all believers to lead a God-glorifying life. The easiest thing in the world is to produce 'little Pharisees' who seem to do and say the right things but aren't really living God-honouring lives. But if we teach the

God-glorifying life of Christ, the moral lives of our young people will be anchored upon the right foundation.

Young people's moral lives should not be governed by 'do's and don'ts', but instead moulded by the character of God as revealed in His relationship with and towards sinful people.

- We must call our children and young people to be holy because of God's awesome acts of judgment towards His people, His Son, and eventually the whole world. We are to be separate from the world because God's people always have been, from the time of Noah, Abraham, Israel and then Jesus and His first disciples.

- We are loving towards a sinful and rebellious world because God has always acted with love and mercy towards sinners, from the time of Adam to Israel and then in Christ to the whole world.

- We are to hate idolatry in the world, and especially among His people, because God has always been seen to hate idolatry in the world, but especially among His people.

Teaching the Bible this way should mould young people whose lives are being morally conformed by the character of God, and not by anything else.

d. Relationships built through teaching the Word

The best way to build relationships is by teaching the Word of God. As we share God's Word, our aim is to follow Paul's example found in 1 Thessalonians 2 v 8-13, and to be a spiritual father and mother to children and young people. As the group and leaders are presented with God's Word, the effect is that God's Word begins to change their hearts.

One of the biggest and most heart-warming effects is that they begin to reflect God's love for the lost. Our responsibility as youth and children's leaders, therefore, must be to provide an environment where they can bring their friends to hear the gospel clearly proclaimed.

The key is for the young disciples and the leaders to be doing this as a **team**. So it's not just the young people reaching their friends, or the leaders reaching the young people's friends, but both reaching their friends together.

Reaching friends

1. Solid foundation
What is it that makes a group like this distinctively Christian?

a. It must be run by Christians who are seeking, with the Holy Spirit's help, to be as holy as they can.

b. Hearing God's voice must be the hub from which everything else gets its meaning and purpose. The shape the evening takes, and what we choose to do or not do, will reflect this.

2. Exposing the lies of the world we live in
The aim of the teaching is to unleash the Word of God upon the world that our young people are living in. When this is your aim, you'll see God's Word exposing the lies of our culture. This produces two effects:

1. **The unbeliever:** The first effect is upon the non-Christian. As the Word of God exposes the lies that they love, follow and believe in, it calls them to true repentance and back to God.

2. **The Christian:** It encourages them hugely. All week they have been struggling with the lies of their culture and the struggle of living in an ungodly world. But now they see those lies exposed by the Word of God. For once in their

week they can stand tall, realising that true enjoyment is to be found in obedience to God and His Word.

Here is a talk outline and some discussion group questions that you might use at an evangelistic meeting:

WHO'S UP THE TREE?—LUKE 19

Teaching Aim

- To show that Jesus loves sinful people and offers them forgiveness.

- If we think only nice people get to heaven, then we have never understood the message and mission of Jesus.

Talk Outline

1. He's greedy—Luke 19 v 1-4

a. Zac has the nasty knack of making loads of stack (money), and he doesn't care how. He ain't frightened of no one, everyone hates him, but no one dare touch him.

b. He's heard rumours of Jesus, and he wants in; he wants to see this miracle worker, and stunning speaker.

2. He's gobsmacked—Luke 19 v 5-6

a. Jesus stops and looks—everyone is waiting for Jesus to let rip, but... No. Instead He walks off to Zac's shack.

---

3. They're gutted—Luke 19 v 7

a. The response of those looking on is utter disgust, and confusion.

b. How could any one want to be with Zac?

c. How could the holy man want to be with him?

d. Jesus is not what they thought Him to be (Luke 19 v 10-12).

4. He's grateful—Luke 19 v 8-10

a. Tea and cake and the Zac attack. Jesus reveals to Zac that He knows all about his mean-minded, money-grabbing life style.

b. In one sense this is nothing new—everyone knew about it. But Jesus seemed to really know Zac, and it worried him silly.

c. Zac heard about God's anger with selfish people, and how they deserved punishment from God. Zac realised he was doomed.

d. But then Jesus said the most beautiful words to Zac (Luke 19 v 10), and then Zac knew he had hope. God loved him and could forgive him.

e. Now that his relationship with God was right, he wanted to put his relationship with others right, too.

Discussion Group Questions

1. Why were the people so shocked and angry that Jesus wanted to spend time with Zacchaeus? Look up Luke 19 v 1-7.

2. Does it surprise you that Jesus wanted to spend time with people like Zacchaeus? Explain why or why not.

3. In what way does this show that they clearly did not understand the mission and message of Jesus? Look up Luke 19 v 9.

4. Why did Zacchaeus change his life so radically? Look up Luke 19 v 8.

5. If you are, or you want to become, a Christian, how might your life radically change?

Conclusion

This chapter gives a few suggestions for ways to 'let the lion loose' in your group. The aim is to create an environment where God's Word is let loose to save souls and mould disciples who love Christ.

God's wonderful Word doesn't need defending. If we 'let it loose', God will graciously work through it in the lives of our children and young people.

Trevor Pearce is a full-timer who manages a large youth-work team at the Bridge Chapel, Liverpool. He specialises in 11-14s. Trevor is married to Eva, and has three daughters. He is passionate about West Ham.

7. Serving suggestions

How do we encourage teenagers to get serving?

I'M A BIG FAN of good food. After all, you don't get to be 6'4"
tall without being able to sniff out a good meal. But however
much Jamie Oliver & co. might carry on about the joy that is
contained within a perfectly cooked aubergine, food in the end
is functional. We eat it to bring life, health and growth. But just
as you think that you've just been given the perfect excuse to
order a giant pizza, here's the catch—to do that it must be com-
bined with exercise. Good food and exercise are as inseparable
as roast beef and horseradish, or apple pie and custard.

The apostle Paul knew that what is true for our flesh and
bones is equally as true for God's people, the body of Christ.
Ephesians 4 v 11-12 tells us that Christ gave apostles, prophets
and pastor teachers who would feed God's people with God's
Word, but feed them so that they would be prepared to serve.
Good food and exercise is how 'the whole body, joined and

held together by every supporting ligament, grows and builds itself up in love, as each part does its work' (Ephesians 4 v 16).

If our young people are going to grow into maturity in Christ, they must be getting regular exercise; that is, they must be serving. So let me ask you: Is your youth work breeding a generation of couch potatoes? Are your young people weekly filling up on the best food, but in danger of becoming unfit through inactivity?

So what does spiritual exercise look like for a young person? Where are the opportunities to serve? Is there more to it than a procession of teenagers handing out hymnbooks and making endless cups of tea?

If our young people are to get serving, they will need to understand at least three things:

1. A love for God's people is the mark of God's family

In chapter 3 of John's first letter, he shows how we can distinguish between the children of God and the children of the devil (1 John 3 v 9-10). In v 14, John sums up what he has been saying: 'We know that we have passed from death to life because we love our brothers'. Love for our Christian brothers and sisters is the identifying mark of the children of God.

Christian service begins with service within the church. The question then must be: How can your young people demonstrate love for the people of God? It could be assisting in the children's groups or the crèche on Sunday morning. It could be babysitting (and not charging!) to allow parents the chance to attend a church event, or have a much-needed night out together. Our group has used the half-term holiday to go and serve teas and chat to the members of our older people's ministry. It could be that out of love for God's people your young people could brave the church prayer meeting. After all, what better way is there to express a love for the people of God than to pray for the life and ministry of the church?

To clarify things further, John draws the contrast with Cain, whose wrong attitude to God (1 John 3 v 12b) boiled over into anger and then violence towards his brother (v 12a). John's point is that rivalry and competition are completely opposed to a life marked by love for God's family.

Yet how often do those attitudes creep into the service we offer, and how often do the ideas for service that we suggest to our young people place them in situations where they are likely to fall prey to these temptations? So often the service projects that we suggest are 'in the spotlight', rather than 'behind the scenes', be that playing music in church services, helping run holiday clubs, or leading in a youth-group meeting.

Of course, none of these are wrong. In fact, they are all wonderful opportunities for young people to grow and build up the body of Christ. However, they also all increase the temptation for the young person to make a show of their own righteousness, to compare themselves to others, and even to look down on those not involved in such high-profile aspects of church life.

How much better to encourage opportunities to serve behind the scenes, to show love when no one is watching? Putting away the chairs at the end of a meeting; washing up after a Christianity Explored meal; or meeting with a housebound pensioner to listen to a recording of the Sunday service. Service behind the scenes exposes the underlying motivation, and the motivation that identifies a young person as a child of God is a love for God's people.

Such love is not easy—it is extremely costly—but that is the standard that Jesus set:

> This is how we know what love is: Jesus Christ laid down his life
> for us. And we ought to lay down our lives for our brothers.
> **1 John 3 v 16**

Just as Cain's hatred led to murder, Jesus' love led to sacrifice. Our response to the salvation that Christ's love bought for us is that we must love our brothers and sisters in the same way. John illustrates the cost this entails with the example of using our material possessions to meet needs within the family of God (v 17).

Getting our young people to serve in this way could be as simple as encouraging them to be generous with the lending of their DVDs and games consoles. It could be establishing a giving project—but from experience something that is local, tangible, and limited in time is more realistic than a long-term commitment, where initial enthusiasm and ownership can be hard to sustain, and often falls back on the leaders, rather than the young people themselves.

Of course, material needs are not the only ones that are costly to meet. John makes the point that the principle is one of action, not words (v 18). There's no point saying we love our brothers and sisters, if we fail to do anything to back that up.

One way of encouraging action could be a 'talent auction'— although for various reasons, not least child protection, encouraging small groups, rather than individuals, to offer a service might be a better way to run one of these.

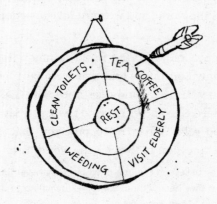

Another option that we have experimented with is having a regular slot in our meetings which we've called 'the Random Service Generator'. This is a rather grand name for what is effectively a Bull's-eye style dartboard, except 'iiiiiinnnnn one' is a service project rather than a food processor! Each group throws a dart and whatever it lands on, that's what they have to do. However you choose to do it, loving God's people means getting on and doing something, not just talking about it.

But why this focus on the church? Are Christians not to love the world? Are we not to serve our communities and our unbelieving friends? This brings us to the second thing our young people must understand if they are to get serving.

2. The cross of Jesus is the mark of God's love for the world

Encouraging young people to get involved with serving their communities, through service projects like litter collections, removing graffiti, painting parties etc. has become hugely popular. We owe a debt to initiatives to such as Oasis' *Faithworks* and Soul Survivor's *Noise* projects, for helping youth groups rediscover this passion for loving the communities in which we live. God loves the world, and we must love in actions, not just in words.

But ultimately, God loved the world so much that 'He sent his one and only Son into world that we might live through him' (1 John 4 v 9). The world does not know God, and people's greatest need is to know that God has sent a Saviour to rescue them. God calls Christians to proclaim that message as their greatest expression of love for the world. For:

> How can they believe in the one of whom they have not heard?
> And how can they hear without someone preaching to them? ...
> As it is written, 'How beautiful are the feet of those who bring good news!' (Romans 10 v 14-15)

There is a great temptation to hide behind words like those of Francis of Assisi, that we must 'preach the gospel always, when necessary use words'. The temptation is to think that our actions will speak on their own—but if we are to love and serve the world, we must use words in order to tell our communities of the good news of God's Saviour.

So, if we are to get our young people serving the world, we must use our youth groups to equip them to tell others the gospel. Evangelism training needs to be a regular part of our programmes, helping them to be familiar with a gospel summary and giving them some pointers as to how to answer tough questions. Another regular feature should be opportunities to support each other in the encouragements and frustrations of trying to tell others about the Lord Jesus.

In *Changing the World,* Ken Moser suggests including an item called 'Flag' in meetings to give a chance for young people to tell the rest of the group of a time that they have raised their Christian colours and spoken out for Jesus. This has been a real encouragement in our group.

Finally, why not organise opportunities for teenagers to be involved in evangelism alongside older Christians. During a parish visiting project in Harold Wood, it was great to see young people pairing up with an adult member of the church to go and offer a gospel video to houses in the parish. In a similar way, the community service projects mentioned earlier can become great training exercises in talking about Jesus, so that young people are equipped to serve those they meet by telling them the good news.

Of course, in the end it is God Himself who equips His people for service, and that is the third thing that young people need to understand if they are to get serving.

3. The gifts of the Spirit are the mark of God's equipping

The demand to love other Christians as Christ loved the church, and to love the world by telling people of the Lord Jesus' death for them, could very easily leave any Christian feeling powerless and defeated. This is no less true for young people.

---

* Ken Moser. *Changing the World through Christian Youth Work,* 2004. Available through The Good Book Company.

It is a great encouragement then to turn to 1 Peter because that letter was written to Christians who, despite facing 'all kinds of trials' (1 Peter 1 v 6), were being called to 'love one another deeply' (1 Peter 4 v 8) and at the same time to 'always be prepared to give an answer to everyone who asks you to give the reason for the hope that you have' (1 Peter 3 v 15). As Peter encouraged them to get serving, he made sure to remind them that every Christian should use the gift that God had given them (1 Peter 4 v 10).

Spiritual gifts seem to be a constant source of discussion and confusion among Christians, but Peter has two simple things to say that should be both a great encouragement and a great motivation to get young people serving. The first is that God gives gifts to administer grace.

1 Peter 4 v 10 makes it clear that spiritual gifts are given to 'each one', not to high fliers. Every Christian has been given

gifts by God, so they are not just for 'proper' Christians, or 'spiritual' Christians, or older Christians. Any young person who has become a Christian has spiritual gifts. This is not Advanced-Level Christianity!

What's more, these gifts are given to 'serve others', not to serve ourselves. Spiritual gifts are given for a purpose, and that purpose is to enable us to show love to those around us. Yet so often, there is a temptation to use them for our own benefit. Either we see them as a means of winning respect from those around us, or we see them as a way to fulfil our own potential. Neither of these are why they are given, and our young people need to understand that, if they are to avoid the temptation to serve out of rivalry.

So what are these gifts? Well, they are given in 'various forms' (1 Peter 4 v 10), not to make us all the same. They are as varied as God's grace itself which, of course, is as different as all the different situations that we face. God gives to His people a variety of gifts, so that together we can serve people in their various needs.

As youth leaders, we need to be very careful not to suggest that we all ought to be the same. Some churches have sadly sometimes given that impression when they have suggested that, for instance, everyone ought to be teaching the Bible, as though that was the only gift that was really valuable. Others might emphasise speaking in tongues, as though we are missing out if that is not our gift. If that is the message our young people hear, all it will achieve is a large number of teenagers feeling inadequate and unable to serve. Gifts aren't given to make us all the same; they are given to help all Christians love and serve others.

As a youth leader, it will therefore be important for you to be involved in helping young people identify their gifts. This will mean encouraging them into areas of service that you feel they would be most suited to. It will mean giving them opportunities to test out gifts under the watchful eye of a member of the leadership team. It will extend into giving feedback and helping them to develop gifts that you discern that they possess. It will involve helping them to think through how they may use their God-given gifts in serving the people of God as they grow up.

There is, though, another reason why Christians have been given gifts. 1 Peter 4 v 11 tells us that God gives gifts to bring glory to Himself.

It is important that as young people begin to serve, they recognise that, without God, they couldn't do what they are doing. Even in our best moments, when we are being our most loving or our most sacrificial, we have to acknowledge that, whether it is in speaking or in practical service, the ability to serve comes from the giver of the gifts that we are using.

God gives gifts so that His people will praise Him. Praise Him that He is the God who gives. He is the strong one, the speaking one, the loving one, the God who serves His people.

If our young people are to 'become mature, attaining to the whole measure of the fullness of Christ' (Ephesians 4 v 13), then we must encourage them to get serving. We must give them opportunities to unobtrusively show love to God's people, boldly declare God's saving love to the world, and humbly do it all with the gifts and the strength that God provides.

David Whitehouse has just moved his family back to the North West of England so that they can fully benefit from the Peak District, Manchester City Football Club and the liquid sunshine of south Manchester. He is now the Associate Minister for Young People at Cheadle Parish Church.

Bible Study
Read 1 John 3 v 10–18

1. What, according to v 10, is one of the key identifying marks of a child of God? What does this tell us about where we should initially focus our service?

2. When we consider the way we serve others, how does the description of Cain in v 12 act as a model to avoid?

3. In what way do John's comments in v 17, about how we serve others with our possessions, connect the example of Jesus in v 16 with the demand for actions, not words, in v 18?

Read 1 Peter 4 v 7–11

4. Why, according to v 10, is it important that our young people have a correct understanding of spiritual gifts if they are going to serve?

5. Why does v 11 say it is essential that Christians serve in the strength that God provides?

CASE STUDY

What Katie did...

Katie Luff is 16, and a regular member of her church youth group. A year ago, members of the group were encouraged to start helping with the Sunday morning children's groups. Katie was keen to get involved, and volunteered to help with the 3-5s. This was initially intended to be once a term—but Katie enjoyed it so much it soon became full time!

Why does Katie do it? She says, 'It's great fun. It's good hearing their answers and views of Christianity. It helps you think about how you think about God.'

Katie has really enjoyed passing on her own knowledge. She finds that teaching the Bible to young children affirms that she believes it herself, and that she wants to pass that message on to others. She's also learned how much work goes into teaching the Bible at this level!

What would Katie say to another teenager who's thinking about serving in this way? 'Go for it! It's great fun, and you've got nothing to lose. I didn't know that I loved working with children. Now I'm hoping to do it full time. My service to God is this way—but there are other ways to serve God. Give it a go and see what's right for you.'

8. Out of control?

How can we keep effective discipline?

OUR AIM IN THIS BOOK has been to help children's and youth leaders to be Bible-centred in the work they do. We did a survey of the questions asked by leaders at a series of Big Issue training days*, and then aimed to give biblical answers to the top ten questions. Which brings us to the subject of discipline—one of the most frequently asked questions of all. It seems that every leader either struggles with discipline themselves, or knows someone who does!

It would be easy to think that the rest of this book focuses on teaching the Bible faithfully, while this chapter is purely practical. But effective discipline matters because, without it, we would not be able to teach the Bible at all!

---

* See the appendix on page 156 for information about the *Big Issue* training series.

Three Principles

In this chapter we're going to look at the subject of discipline under three principles:

1. Discipline is a TEAM issue

Discipline is never just the responsibility of the person at the front. It is always a team issue. This is why you will find regular 'Team Talk' sections throughout this chapter.

2. Discipline is a PLANNING issue

Loss of discipline can often be traced back to poor planning. Instead, we need to plan our sessions in such a way as to avoid or minimise possible discipline problems.

3. Discipline is a GOSPEL issue

We are in a life-changing work, which has eternal consequences. So effective discipline matters. Otherwise our young people may lose opportunities to hear the great news about Jesus Christ.

1. Discipline is a TEAM issue

I used to be an assistant leader in a cub pack. One year we took the cubs away to camp at a site that included a large wooden hut. This hut could be used for activities when the weather was bad, but had a very strict rule that no ball games were allowed inside it.

One afternoon I had the boys gathered together at one end of the hut, while I explained a treasure hunt that had been set up round the site. The treasure hunt was well planned, and was going to be a great deal of fun. But it was extremely difficult to get the boys to listen quietly while I gave them their instructions. Why? Because the rest of the leaders were at the other end of the hut playing football! They were noisy, distracting, and demonstrating to the cubs that rules are made to be broken. No wonder I had a discipline problem!

Most of us work in some kind of team, even if a rota system means the team is different each week. So how can we support one another, to help reduce or avoid discipline problems?

- **Discipline is never** just the responsibility of the person at the front. Sometimes it will be appropriate for that person to bring a child back on task by speaking to them from the front, but at most other times this will be an unhelpful distraction.

- **You need to agree between you** how you will handle discipline as a team. For example, if one leader is doing a talk at the front, but one or two young people keep interrupting, who will handle the situation and how will they go about it? The whole team needs to be clear about this.

- **Always do what you say you will do.** Don't make empty threats. (This means you have to think through your 'threats' first!). Don't make empty promises either. Always do what you say you will do.

I recently heard a mother tell her son several times 'I'll just be a minute', when I knew (and so did she!) that she would be at least ten. Whenever possible, think through what you will say before you say it, so that you can be accurate and truthful. If you do realise that you've given unrealistic expectations to your young people, apologise to them and then give them the real, accurate version.

The aim is to build a relationship where they know that you mean what you say, and that you will be honest with them. (As well as being vital for effective discipline, this models to your group that Christians speak the truth—just as the God we serve is always true, and always means what He says.)

- **Be consistent** as a team in your expectations. Don't let them play one leader off against another. (But if this does happen, work out the best way forward and then be honest with the children about it.) This means you will need to agree on behaviour expectations between you, and then make sure that the whole team knows what they are (and that the young people do too!) Be realistic and fair about your expectations. ('Don't exasperate your children', Ephesians 6 v 4.) There are some sample expectations in the case study on page 106.

- **Talk about discipline issues** when debriefing after a session. Don't just focus on what went wrong—encourage each other about what went right too!

- **Keep other team members informed** (eg: if two children have fallen out, or a dad has left home.) These are the kind of issues that may lead to a sudden change in behaviour—

and that you need to know about anyway. If you have a rota system, think about how you will pass on this kind of information to others in the team.

- **Pray together** for the children or young people in your group—especially for any you struggle to like. It has been my experience that praying regularly for someone changes how I feel about them. As I pray, I recognise God's love for that person; His good and loving plans for them; and my own inability to do anything of eternal value without His help. This doesn't make a difficult youngster easy to love, but I have found that it makes a huge difference to my attitude towards them.

TEAM TALK

Because discipline is a team issue, we suggest that you meet with the rest of your team and try to establish an agreed pattern of working together. The questions below will help.

Discuss the role of each team member in maintaining effective discipline. If a child is being disruptive, who will respond first, and how? Will this be the same person each week? Will it depend on the gender of the child? Will you go and sit with the young person, or move them? If you move them, where to?

Discuss any young people in your group who particularly struggle in their behaviour. What strategies have you found to be effective? Are there other youngsters who tend to set them off? How can you ensure that you give love and encouragement to this young person—and not just focus on bad behaviour.

---

2. Discipline is a PLANNING issue

As a young leader on a Beach Mission team, I went along to an evening event to see what was happening. The young people had been sat in rows on a hard wooden floor, ready to watch a filmstrip. (Ouch—that shows my age!!!) The projector wasn't working, so the two leaders at the front turned their backs on the group and started fiddling with the projector. This went on for ten minutes, during which time the young people were left with nothing to do. Not surprisingly, a large number of them took this as an opportunity to mess around!

Not all discipline problems arise because of planning issues—but a significant number of them do. The following suggestions should help to reduce that number:

- **Children and young people are not adults.** (Although adults are often disruptive in sessions too!) Plan realistically for their level of understanding, likely attention span, their need to use up energy etc. If you don't know much about child development, get help to find out what's realistic for the age group you work with. You will find helpful summaries in some youth-work books, or ask an experienced leader or teacher to come to a team meeting to talk with you about it.

- **If you have youngsters with known special needs** in your group, plan specifically for them. If you're not sure how, talk it through with their parent or a teacher.

- **Give clear directions** for activities, and ensure all resources are available (and working!). That implies checking everything beforehand, and turning up early enough to set up properly. (Arriving early helps enormously with discipline: you can set up properly; you're available to greet and talk with the children, rather than having your back turned while you set things up; you can build relationships with them; it shows that they matter to you; you can pray beforehand...)

- **Younger children respond well** to a reward scheme that reinforces good behaviour. If you use one, make sure that the team are all consistent in how it is used.

- **Plan your activities** to minimise the risk of hyping them up. If necessary, jettison a favourite game if you think they will run wild. Think about how you will quieten them down after a lively activity.

- **Don't let your planning sheet** become your master. If something isn't working—stop—and change the activity.

- **Your team is a strength**—use it! eg: to have a change of voice to listen to. This will help your young people to keep concentrating. Some team members may be particularly gifted at leading games. Others will be good at leading discussions, or quietly getting alongside shy youngsters. Don't just have other team members sitting in for the whole session—plan to use them.

TEAM TALK

Look back at a session you've just run (or one already planned). Try to draw a graph of the activities, and the effect they will have on your group. (Eg: which activities will excite the group, or even hype them up? Which are quieter or more reflective?)

Now look at the overall shape of the graph. Do you have a wide enough range of activities to keep things moving? Or are the children likely to become bored or restless? What is your longest activity, and is this too long for this age group? Do you have a variety of voices for them to listen to? (Eg: one leader telling the story, another explaining a game.) Where does the main Bible teaching fit into the overall shape? Is it just after a noisy game, or have you given the group an opportunity to quieten down and be ready to listen? Are you giving them every opportunity to hear and understand the great news about Jesus?

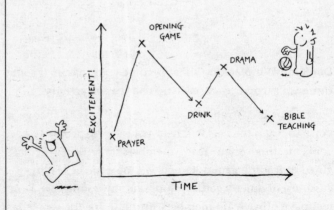

3. Discipline is a GOSPEL issue

- **Christian children's and youth work has eternal consequences**. That's why effective discipline matters. We can't do good Bible teaching if we don't have control of the group. (That's why we need to be willing to remove a disruptive child from the group—temporarily, or possibly even permanently.)

- **We have the opportunity** to model real forgiveness to the young people in our group. (As opposed to the 'partial forgiveness' they may have met elsewhere.)

- **PRAY!!!**—for your young people, for yourself and for the team.

TEAM TALK

Children and young people are sinners just like us, and we can't expect perfect behaviour. However, by working together as a team, and planning our sessions carefully, we can minimise the likelihood of poor behaviour.

But we also need to PRAY! God loves these children and young people far more than we ever can. Ask Him to work in their hearts, so that they can hear His Word to them and respond to Him.

Agree as a team how you will pray for your group. Will you meet together to pray? Will you each commit yourselves to pray for a few children each day? How about producing a team prayer diary? Are there others in your church who can pray too?

CASE STUDY

The following is an example of behaviour expectations for a children's group. Notice that the leaders are expected to behave in the same way!

- Children listen...
  - — when a leader is speaking
  - — when another child is speaking
- Children do what the leader says
- Children help and are kind

- Leaders listen...
  - — when a leader is speaking
  - — when a child is speaking
- Leaders join in with what a leader says
- Leaders help and are kind
- Leaders do what they say (truthful and trustworthy)

When working with younger children, it can be helpful to have these expectations displayed somewhere in your meeting room.

A group of teenagers is unlikely to respond well if you display this kind of list! However, you will still want the same kind of behaviour from them. Discuss as a team the best way to put these expectations across to your group, and remember the impact that team behaviour will have on your group. If two leaders are gossiping in the corner, your teens will see that it's OK for them to do the same.

Bible Study

The way that we act towards the children and young people in our care should reflect the way that God acts towards us. Read the following verses:

1 John 4 v 7-8

Psalm 33 v 4-5

Deuteronomy 32 v 4

Psalm 103 v 8

Joshua 21 v 45

For each verse:

1. What aspect(s) of God's character is shown here?

2. How can we reflect that characteristic in the way we relate to our group?

If we are teaching God's Word faithfully to our group members, we won't ever teach morality for its own sake. Our aim is not to produce well-behaved, moral children— but followers of Christ. A godly life will then develop as God makes them more like His Son. For example: as Christians, we will want to be honest because God is truth; and to be loving because God is love.

3. Look again at the list of characteristics from question 1. How can we encourage the young people in our groups to develop these same character traits?

Alison Mitchell is the Children's Editor at the Good Book Company and is involved with youth training events around the country, including the Big Issue. She now has even more grey hairs than she did when she started editing this book.

9. Poles apart

How do we integrate children and young people into the congregation?

BILLY GROANED as the dreaded cry thundered up the stairs: 'Come on, time for church!' Why couldn't he just be like normal children, who watched television or played sport on a Sunday? Not him, he had to go to that cold and uncomfortable building.

Sandwiched between his Mum and a stranger, he'd have to listen to the incomprehensible mantra of a man in a dress at the front. How that man could go on, and on, and on! Billy had no idea what was said. He did try listening a couple of times, but he couldn't make head nor tail of the language: 'the Scripture moveth us in sundry places to acknowledge and confess our manifold sins and wickedness; and that we should not dissemble nor cloak them blah, blah, blah, blah, blah'.

Billy gave up trying to understand; instead his whole mind was set on surviving the 'Te Dious' and arriving at the second hymn, when at last, he could make his escape and join with his friends in church hall.

Billy is a fictional character, yet his story is a reality for many children and young people today. For them, the experience of church is on a par with being dragged around the local garden centre. It holds no appeal, and there are so many other things they'd rather be doing.

This negative experience inclines them to vote with their feet as soon as they are able[1]. The past few years have seen a number of alarming statistics identifying the exodus of young people from churches in the UK[2]. While there are any number of reasons for their departure, the reality is that, in a significant number of cases, it is the church's method, not the message, that is rejected[3].

---

1 Researcher Peter Brierly identifies that 75% of those who left church did so before they reached 13. *Reaching and Keeping Teenagers*, Brierly 1993 pg 101

2 Brierly calculates that nearly half of the 10-19 year olds attending church in 1979 were no longer doing so by 1989. *ibid.* pg 90

3 'Church is utterly weary and holds nothing of interest' wrote one 13 year old. *ibid.* pg 91

Recent years have seen a pragmatic response to this impending crisis. Many churches now employ full-time youth and children's workers. Youth churches have been established and the market has been flooded with vibrant material for Sunday School teachers to use. All this energy has been expended out of a recognition that today's young people are growing up in a world very different to previous generations, and need to be catered for in a culturally relevant way[4].

While many of these developments are to be welcomed, we should be aware that some carry potentially perilous consequences. The more cultural and personal preferences are accommodated, the more polarisation will occur, and polarisation spawns exclusive subgroups.

Youth churches for example, in their very nature, exclude anyone who isn't a youth. Many youth groups become *de facto* youth churches because their programme runs parallel to the 'main church', to the point that a young person may be thoroughly involved in the group, yet have no experience of the adult congregation.

Unwittingly, youth and children's workers can become catalysts to polarisation by creating strong identities for their groups, separating them from the congregation in the mind of the adults and young people alike.

---

4 In 2004 a Church of England working group published a report entitled *Mission Shaped Church* in which the following observation was made, 'young people are growing up in a different world to that experienced by previous generations. The life experiences of young people in modern industrialised societies have changed significantly over the last two decades'. The conclusion drawn is that young people are not simply a different age, they belong to an entirely different culture group.

I have been guilty of this myself. By establishing a sense of identity for the youth group I run, with their own programme and logo, without thinking, I reinforced in their minds that they belonged there and not the main church family. I have since repented and now refuse to refer to the youth group as anything other than 'our young people'.

The polarisation problem

Why is this such an issue? What's the problem with having the church made up of independent homogeneous units?

Inevitably, our church life will be impoverished if a particular generation is absent. In a congregation of entirely young people, for example, where does the wisdom of the years come from? Where will the example of the life that has persevered be found? How will the younger learn the lessons of history? Polarisation impoverishes the church.

Polarisation also perpetuates the modern attitude that church exists solely for the benefit and entertainment of the individual. Potentially then, if it fails to meet a felt need or makes too great a demand, it will be dropped[5].

The New Testament calls for a radically different approach. In Ephesians 4 the apostle Paul exhorts his readers to 'make every effort to keep the unity of the Spirit' (v 3). Notice that he doesn't urge them to create a unity, but to maintain the unity that already exists. They are one after all:

---

5 The government initiative 'the Tomorrow Project' predicts that in the coming years 'People's expectations of relationships will change. As made-to-measure expectations spread, people will be less inclined to negotiate difficulties and conflicts in a group. If the group doesn't fit me exactly, I'll move on'. *The Tomorrow Project* - Moynagh in Moynagh & Worsley, 2000.

> There is one body and one Spirit—just as you were called to one
> hope when you were called. (Ephesians 4 v 4)

They are one in the gospel—fact. That being the case, their responsibility is to make every effort to live that out, in community, bearing with one another in love. Accommodating the needs of any one group in church life in such a way as to annex them from the body is hardly making every effort!

For the apostle Paul, it was not an option to have a local church consisting of polarised groups. The flow of his letter to the Ephesians addresses this specific issue. There were Jews and there were Gentiles in the church in Ephesus—two more culturally opposed groups you couldn't wish to find—yet they were to work out their church life together because, through the cross, Christ 'has made the two one' (Ephesians 2 v 14).

Here we come to the very core of the issue: more serious than impoverished community life, polarisation impacts the very nature and purpose of the church! We will fail to be the radical organism we are designed to be. We will fail to tell the truth about the gospel!

The big picture

In the garden of Eden, the Fall had disastrous consequences for relationships. Genesis 2 v 25 provides us with a picture of right relationships. Adam and Eve were together, naked and without shame. Immediately after the forbidden fruit was eaten however, we learn that their eyes were opened, enabling them to know their nakedness. By making covering for themselves, they were hiding from one another. The first recorded casualty of the Fall was the relationship between people.

The second was the relationship between the people and God. On hearing the sound of the Lord in the garden, Adam and Eve ducked for cover, hiding from God.

The Fall of man brought fracture to relationships. Since that day, the unfolding chapters of human history have told a sorry tale of dispute and discord, of hate and of hiding.

Come the end of history, however, there's an altogether different scenario! In Revelation 7 we're allowed a snapshot of heaven. There, gathered before the throne of the Lamb, are the assembled people of God, gathered in from across the ages, and, critically for us, from across the divisions of humanity. There, united together in their worship of the Lamb, are every tribe, nation, people and language, a glorious unity of diversity.

What a remarkable difference! Concord has replaced conflict. Reconciliation has replaced rift. Such is the effectiveness of the gospel that all the barriers that kept mankind from God have been overcome. So too, have the barriers that kept one man from another.

This is God's big plan for His world, 'to bring all things in heaven and on earth together under one head, even Christ' (Ephesians 1 v 10). It's an ultimate reality, but it's to be worked out in the life of the church here and now, expressed in the life of the local body.

In chapter 3 of Ephesians, Paul begins to speak about a mystery previously concealed. Through the gospel, the outsiders, the Gentiles, were heirs together with the insiders, the Jews. Never before was it suggested that these two people groups would share the same status and inheritance, but God has designed it thus that 'through the church, the manifold wisdom of God should be made known to the rulers and authorities in the heavenly realms' (Ephesians 3 v 10).

In other words, through the unity of diversity that exists within the new community of Christ, the many splendoured wisdom of God is revealed to the watching heavens! In coming together in this way, united in Christ and by Christ and with Christ, the church demonstrates to the whole of heaven the reversal of the process of alienation introduced by Satan in the garden long ago.

The church is to be a new community, in which the divisions which afflict mankind are eradicated. In so being, the church makes an emphatic statement that the plan of reconciliation has been accomplished, the death of Christ effective and the future certain.

Furthermore, if we take Jesus' prayer to his Father in John 17 into consideration, then we can add an extra dimension to the church's purpose. It is not just to the heavens that she makes a declaration, but to the earth too:

> May they be brought to complete unity to let the world know
> that you sent me and have loved them even as you have loved
> me. (John 17 v 23)

To have a church that is exclusively for one kind of person and not another, fails to tell the truth about the gospel. As Phil Moon and Mark Ashton put it:

> Where a generation barrier appears in the life of a church, it must
> be resisted as strongly as racism or sexism. If we abandon the
> vision of a church without age barriers, we are discarding part of
> the gospel, just as much as if we accept that there should be dif-
> ferent churches for different classes, races or skin colours[7].

Here and now, it is the privilege and responsibility of each local church, as an expression in time and space of the church universal and invisible, to be a unity of diversity. This theology of reconciliation is to be worked out very practically in the church now! Which means that integration of children and young people is not an optional extra; it is essential to the church being what we are called to be.

However, therein lies the problem. How do we express our gospel unity, with all the differences that requires us to encompass, and successfully keep the Billys of this world in church? The answer lies in the very thing that both church and people are made for—relationships!

Countering the culture

Back to Billy. It's Saturday morning. Billy can be found hurriedly tidying his room; the coffee mugs are cleared from under the bed, the clothes are scraped from the floor and the dubious poster comes down from the wall. Why is he going to these

---

7 *Christian Youth Work*, pg 98 Mark Ashton, Authentic 2006.

extreme lengths? His Grandma and Grandad are coming to stay! He's excited. He wants to show off his room because it matters to him what they think.

Billy's grandparents are culturally miles away from where he is. They're into pea pods—he's into iPods. But they're family. He is their flesh and blood. They take an interest in him and they have a relationship with him.

Here's the key. Within the nuclear family unit the cultural and generational gaps are not closed, but they are spanned through significant relationships. Likewise, within the church family, the cultural and generational divides must be spanned through significant relationships.

The critical question to answer when it comes to integration is not: how can we get our age ranges to occupy the same space together? Popular 'all age' services might be a great expression of diversity united, but they offer limited scope for integration.

The phenomena the gospel initiates is more than a coincidence of people in one place. It's the calling of strangers into family—and the ability of the family unit to thrive is directly proportionate to the quality of relationships that exist within it. The critical question is: how can we progress our relationships across the generations?

Working it out

It may sound obvious, but the first step to achieving integration is to teach the nature and purpose of the church throughout the age ranges! There must be an appreciation of the significance of the gospel for human relationships, if a local church is going to achieve the integration of its members.

Are the implications of the gospel for family life explained and promoted? Are the faithful members aware of the extent of their responsibility towards one another? It needs teaching across the board with utmost clarity and persistence. Children, on the whole, are likely to be fed a diet of Bible narrative, but they too need to be given an understanding of church that enables them to grasp exactly what it is that they belong to.

A right understanding of the nature and purpose of church should naturally cultivate an expectation that generation chasms will be spanned. This expectation in turn must be allowed to impact the planning of the church's activity.

That's not to say that every aspect of church life will be appropriate for every age group—let's be clear about that—but when it comes to setting the social calendar, the next mission project, the structure of the meetings, the fund-raising initiatives and so on, it needs to be done with the entire family in mind. What can we do together? In which areas can the generations co-operate and work side by side? What adjustments can be made to accommodate a wider range of people?

So much of our church life takes place in age-specific groupings that work against integration, largely because these kinds of questions are simply not on the agenda of many children's workers, youth leaders and church councils. But if we want to be the integrated church we're called to be, we'd do well to start asking them!

Having taught the priority of cross-generational relationships, and created an environment in which they might flourish, how do we actually initiate the process of establishing them? After all, a young person is hardly likely to march up to an adult and strike up a conversation; they are generally far too self conscious. Younger members can be equally intimidating to older people. All manner of dynamics mitigate against people stepping out of their comfort zones to engage the unknown and different. That's why in many churches up and down the land you can observe the gathering of the like–minded at coffee time.

There are some ideas at the end of this chapter which might help get the ball rolling, but the basic principle is that relationship-building needs to be made as straight forward and least costly as possible, especially in the early stages.

Churches benefit when creative ways into conversation are provided, and in the final analysis, the onus falls on the older, and hopefully more mature, members of the community to take the initiative. They need to be encouraged to demonstrate the self-giving other-centredness that gospel living will produce. The church must look to them to show a striving for unity. If we want our children and young people to embrace the older members, then the older members need to model it to them.

Hopefully, we have seen that the question of integration has far more to do with relationships than coinciding in a particular place. It is far more than the weekly meeting. However, it does include the weekly meeting! Children, especially, can receive the message that this church business is not for them, if there is no attempt to acknowledge and include them in the main expression of church life. Parents can be so concerned with keeping their offspring quiet that they provide them with toys and the like to distract them. While this may achieve that particular objective, it serves to reinforce the idea that the church meeting is an adult activity.

Not only does a tolerant atmosphere need to be cultivated on the part of the adults, but those leading the service would do well to engage the age spread. A simple explanation of what's taking place goes a long way towards accomplishing this. Some churches even go to the extent of providing child-friendly orders of service designed to inform and include the younger members.

Paying attention to the 'all together' time is even more of an issue where churches operate a structure of Sunday School that sees younger members dismissed to their own age groups in the early stages of the meeting. Traditionally, this system sees them planted in crèche and then on into junior groups, until they reach the early stages of adulthood when the dedicated youth activity switches to the evening. Until that point, they may never have taken a place in the full adult meeting and can find themselves thoroughly unequipped for it. Perhaps it's no coincidence that this is the point when the drop-off occurs most frequently.

A critical examination of the strategy of the young people's work and the structure of the adult meeting is a worthwhile exercise. Are there ways in which the graduation into adult life

CASE STUDY

Ann proved to be a consistent and keen member of the youth group. In time, she began to demonstrate a gift for singing. This was recognised by the church leadership and she was encouraged to take her place in leading the singing in the congregational worship. Her increase in profile made her more approachable to the older members of the church, as they were able to express their appreciation of her service. In time, she was able to strike up a relationship with one of the elderly members, who she proceeded to visit on a regular basis. This blossoming friendship was beneficial for both parties; Ann was a source of encouragement and help while, at the same time, receiving wisdom and support from her more experienced friend. This relationship has continued to flourish long after Ann left the church for university. What a great spectacle for the watching world to behold, two people from opposite ends of the age spectrum with apparently nothing in common in worldly terms, enjoying a significant relationship. This is the fruit of the reconciling gospel.

Hamish is a keen member of the youth group, attending his small-group meeting with consistency. In the context of that group, he was encouraged by his leaders to attend the monthly prayer meeting. Nothing in that meeting would hold any appeal to a teenage boy—a group of predominantly older people gathering to do nothing other than to pray and sing praise. Yet because of the prompting he received, and the example he was set by his leaders, Hamish was even prepared to forgo a Champions League fixture featuring his beloved football team. His sense of priority and commitment warmed the heart of many of the older members, and his participation in the prayer life of the church was a great encouragement to him in his own discipleship.

can be made smoother? One church operates a shorter youth activity, that sees the younger teens leave the meeting only for the duration of the sermon. In this time, they're taken through a syllabus that introduces and explains the various elements of the service, aiming to equip them to take their place in it.

Finally, we need to allow our young people and children to make a contribution to the life of the church. Again in Ephesians, Paul writes of the gifts the risen Jesus has entrusted to the church, gifts which when effectively employed will build up the church (cf. Ephesians 4 v 11). There is no indication that the works of service produced by these gifts are restricted to those over eighteen! It stands to reason then, that as we teach our children and young people they will grow into service. Indeed, Paul suggests that where each person is playing their part, integration will flourish (v16).

So, one of the greatest catalysts to integration is to use the gifts of children and young people in the service of the church family. This is also a great way to cultivate right attitudes and provoke maturity. As well as helping to give young people some responsibility, significance and ownership, looking out for the needs of others orientates them towards a giving mentality.

Of course, for this to happen, we need to encourage, equip and entrust the younger generations with proper roles, and not fob them off or patronise them with a mickey mouse chore to keep them quiet. They'll be the first to pick up on whether they are being genuinely used, as opposed to simply being catered for. The task is important and the equipping is equally so. Like anyone, young people need to be trained, which is an opportunity in itself to get alongside them in the kind of mentoring capacity that has the faint ring of a New Testament precedent (Paul and Timothy for example)!

Perhaps the reason many possible service outlets are closed to children and young people is because it is simply easier to get an adult to do it; they are more reliable after all. Employing the gifts of a younger member might require a bit more organisation, but it will pay dividends all round. Time spent creatively thinking through avenues of service is well spent.

Children can do all manner of things working alongside the adults, from welcoming to playing in the music group to helping with prayers to serving cake. That word 'alongside' is key. All too often the young people are put on a rota and asked to take their turn. Far more effective is using them in conjunction with the adults. Not only does this provide some welcome security, but it facilitates interaction, the key ingredient of integration!

It's not just about the congregational meeting—there are so many elements of church life beyond Sunday that young people particularly can get involved in. Perhaps the most useful is when young people are involved alongside the adults in the mission of the church. According to Jesus' words in John 17, that will make quite an impact on those looking on!

In summary

There is no such thing as a fail-safe recipe for success; we are but sinners, our relationships will not be perfect. We will not be on earth all that we will be in heaven. However, we can begin to point towards it as we unite together across the generations and cultures. The integrated congregation will have: a theological grasp of who and what the church is in Christ; a sign of the barrierless, reconciled community of God's people; an appreciation that unity is achieved in interaction across the generations; and will operate a mindset that longs for, and actively seeks to encourage, relationships that flourish across the boundaries and barriers of our fallen world.

Integration is not the easiest way to grow the church, but it's the best. The integrated church tells the truth about the gospel to the host of heaven and the watching world. The integrated church enables people to be all that they can be; after all, we are made in the image of the God of relationship, the God who is Himself a unique unity of diversity, the source of other–centred love.

The integrated church, by the grace of God, just might see young people like Billy staying put, even in the difficult years, because it wouldn't just be a dull pattern of worship that he'd be walking out on were he to leave. It would be a community he was deserting—a community in which he has a place, a role, a confidence, a security, an acceptance, an identity, a home. If we get integration right, it wouldn't simply be an organisation that Billy felt a part of, it would be a family; not just any family, but the awesome, barrierless, reconciled family of God!

IN PRACTICE—SEVEN IDEAS

1. **The sofa of tranquillity:** One feature of our youth meeting has become known as 'the sofa of tranquillity'. This is a suitably informal setting for an interview with a member of the church family. Not only is the dialogue itself revealing and useful, but the young people are consistently getting a message about the value of the adult congregation. Openings are created for interaction at a later date and the adult congregation gain an insight into the youth meeting, helping to prevent it becoming a private and mysterious offshoot.

2. **Guess who:** One fun idea to get the older and younger interacting, and therefore on the road to building relationships, takes the form of a quiz. We asked a large number of people in the congregation to tell us one significant fact about themselves; these were collated together to form a list. Participants had to put names to statements. It was a great way of enabling the ice to be broken and for introductions to be made. This was further supplemented with photographs of various church family members, taken when they were very young. Again, identifying the various pictures became something of an easy talking point.

3. **Communication:** This is a big issue in many churches. The family members simply do not know what each other are up to! Informing the adults about the activity and progress of the younger members, and vice versa, opens up all manner of opportunities for prayer and conversation. Again, we need the mindset that church is family, and to actively work to prevent any age range functioning without regard for the others. So, in the announcements

in the meeting, reveal or introduce the teaching theme the children will be looking at. It needn't take long. It involves the young and informs the older, providing a talking point. In the youth meeting, go through the church notices (not just the young people's stuff), then get them praying for the full breadth of age groups.

4. **Home groups:** Small-group work is a key part of the life of many churches. Within these it is not necessarily appropriate to have a spread of ages. However, that doesn't prevent the adult homegroup 'sponsoring' a pair of young people, covenanting to pray for them, enquiring of their progress and so forth. It's a structured way of building relationships. At worst, the young people get prayed for; at best, deep and lasting bonds are established across the generations.

5. **Eat:** One thing everybody can do, needs to do and enjoys doing, is eating! One of the best ways to express our family life is round the table. Whether its a 'bring and share' buffet (watch out for mountains of quiche though—why do Christians insist on quiche?) or a catered affair, meal times are a great way to be together. You can even introduce icebreakers and tasks for diners; for example, find out five things you didn't know about the person on your left, then swap seats for dessert and do it again!

6. **Events:** The glorious summer months afford great opportunities for church family events. Picnics in the park with a game of rounders to follow, country walks and treasure hunts, the list goes on. In the winter, get your thinking caps on; quiz nights in mixed teams, even Barn Dances work a treat (although the young people might/will need persuading, they'll have a ball once they are there). There

are a couple of important things to remember when considering church events. Ideally, they need to be accessible to a broad span of age groups. It's worth pondering whether they will facilitate integration or simply allow people to occupy the same space. An event is not an end in itself. It is always to promote family life. A lot of time and effort can be put into an event which is self defeating in its very make up. Timing, cost and nature of an activity are all key considerations.

7. **Create an inroad:** Why not end the formal aspect of the meeting with a challenge: 'Over coffee talk to someone younger than you about…' This simple exercise maintains the expectation of interaction, while opening up an obvious opportunity; even better if it's based on something the congregation has been learning about.

Discussion questions

1. Is there a healthy attitude among and towards the various age groups in your church family? How might this be cultivated / furthered?

2. How does your current church set–up help to promote cross-generational relationships? What are the obstacles? Are there adjustments that can better facilitate interaction?

3. What activities easily lend themselves to including the age spread? Which exclude particular age groups by their nature, timing or cost? Are changes appropriate?

4 What opportunities for service lend themselves to the younger age groups? How can they be encouraged to get involved alongside the adults? What support systems need to be put in place? Bear in mind your church's child protection policy.

Bible Study

Read Ephesians 4 v 1-16

1. How does Paul expect his readers to live a life worthy of the calling they have received? What's involved in 'bearing with one another in love' and 'making every effort'? Why is this so necessary?

2. What is the purpose of the gifts the risen Christ has bestowed on the church? What fruit can be expected? What is required for it to blossom?

3. In v 16 Paul speaks of the whole body moving towards maturity 'as each part does its work'. How does this challenge our expectations of young people and the idea that children are the church of tomorrow?

4. From this passage, what do you think Paul's attitude would be towards polarised groups existing within a local church? Why? How might this motivate you to strive for integration?

Chris Slater has been involved in local church youth ministry long enough to have pulled out a significant percentage of his hair! He loves sport, Hondas, Apple Macs and whatever's in the fridge. Prior to youthwork, he was a graphic designer and at time of writing, he is being institutionalised... in theological college, training to become a vicar. He has promised to continue to do youth-work until he becomes Archbishop of Canterbury.

10. Bridging the gap

How can we build bridges with parents?

'LIFE'S BEEN SO MANIC OF LATE we haven't fed the kids for a week!' If we're so good at providing for our children's physical needs, why are we so good at neglecting their spiritual health?

Wiping bottoms, mucking out bedrooms, getting tea, helping with homework, giving lifts, keeping the peace... the list goes on. Children are a great blessing but they're also jolly hard work, and very easy for Christian parents in the muddle of family life to neglect their greatest responsibility—to bring their children up to know and love the Lord Jesus for themselves.

Of course, many parents won't know it's their responsibility because they've never been told. Those who do know will be all too aware of their failings and the feelings of guilt. They need to be supported and encouraged in this area of Christian family life.

It's a sad fact that most parents will wake up one day to discover their influence over their children has all but disappeared—friends in the playground now occupying the place they once did. That's not to say it's been lost altogether and the relationship won't develop into something special in adulthood, but truths learned as a child can be the most enduring.

So it's never too early to start, and developing good habits from the very beginning has got to be encouraged.

But, just as important, parents need to know and hear that it's never too late to make a start either.

So the principle is simple:

It is the parents' responsibility—with God's grace—to bring their children up to know and love the Lord Jesus for themselves.

Teaching parents the... WHY

Why is it the parents' responsibility? The answer is both *simple* and *obvious*.

Simple because it is a command of God:

> Hear O Israel: The LORD our God, the LORD is one. Love the LORD your God with all your heart and with all your soul and with all your strength. These commandments that I give you today are to be upon your hearts. Impress them on your children. Talk about them when you sit at home and when you walk along the road, when you lie down and when you get up...'
> (Deuteronomy 6 v 4–7)

Tennis club and ballet lessons may be optional extras; teaching our children Christ is not. It is a command of God and, as with all of God's commands, it is for our good and to be obeyed. This passage tells us we are to teach, not only *who the Lord is,* but also *what our response should be*—that of undivided devotion.

And it's **obvious** because no one loves a child more than mum and dad. Of all the things a Christian parent could want for their children, surely eternal life has to be number one; and therefore, teaching Jesus as Lord and Saviour must begin in the home.

The idea that we can leave the spiritual development of our children to the youth and children's workers at church has to be buried once and for all; it is far too important a job to be left to anyone else.

Teaching parents the... HOW

The way we feed our children is no different from the way we feed ourselves, with a regular diet of Bible reading and prayer. We get to know God exactly the same as with any relationship, listening to Him as He speaks through His Word, the Bible, and speaking to Him in prayer—the main difference being we can't see Him as we can one another.

It's this regular diet that breathes life into our relationship with God, and will motivate parents to take the spiritual welfare of their children seriously. Unless mum and dad are excited about Jesus, and growing in their knowledge and love of Him, what chance have they of exciting their children?

So, we need first to be encouraging parents to invest time and energy in their own walk with God. They need to model the joy of knowing and following the Lord at all times and especially in the home, that place where, sadly, the sinful-self most readily bubbles to the surface. It is hard work.

Jesus should be brought into the home in such a way that He becomes part of the family. '...when you sit at home...' suggests perhaps a formal time of Bible reading and prayer when the family sets aside a few minutes each day. Despite all the pressures upon them, Christian fathers must be encouraged to take the lead in this.

The way this is done, either together or alone, will change as children grow, but the earlier this habit is learned, the more chance it will have of surviving turbulent teenage years and into adulthood. There are a number of excellent resources available to help develop and encourage these daily disciplines*.

'Talk about them—talk about Him!—when you walk along the road...' points to the way to enjoy Jesus as we go about the day, and perhaps earth some of the lessons learnt from the Bible.

- There are plenty of excellent Christian CDs that can ease the trauma of a long car journey and provoke discussion.

- 'Twenty things we can thank God for' is another great game for the car.

- Thinking about what Jesus would make of a situation at school, or in the news, at meal times or on the walk to or

---

* See the appendix on page 156 for details of Bible-reading resources for families.

home from school, are other great ways to obey this command.

Jesus is Lord of everything and everyone, and He is to be taught and enjoyed as such. With a little bit of imagination, He can be brought into every part of family life (without encouraging our children to become 'religious nutters' of course!)

And as we seek to teach and model a life of prayer, we mustn't limit our prayers to set times (Bible reading, bed time

or giving thanks at meals). Spontaneous prayers, giving thanks for good news or a good time, for example, for help in times of difficulty, for safety when setting out on a journey, all help teach our children what a living relationship with our heavenly Father looks like.

So far we've assumed that there are two parents in the home and both are Christian, but we know that's not always the case. We need to be wise and sensitive in supporting families, treating each individually, and where there is no Christian influence in the home, then Christian godparents and grandparents etc. should be encouraged in their responsibilities, not least in carrying the burden of prayer.

It can be a great means of outreach too. Asking for help with lifts, or use of the front room for meetings, can be a great way to develop relationships and win the trust of non-Christian parents. Most parents are thrilled when anyone takes a healthy interest in their children, so we shouldn't limit our work with parents to just those who are Christian.

If the world hates Jesus (John 15 v 18), it follows that the pressures on our children to be ashamed or embarrassed about Him will be great. That's why what goes on in the home is so important. We've established that it's first the parents' responsibility to nurture their children in Christ—but the youth and children's workers can play a great supporting role in this, as we'll now see.

Supporting parents in their responsibility

Resources may be limited, ideas need never be. You may not have a full-time youth worker, but that doesn't mean things at church can't be organised to give parents the maximum support possible. Some of the following ideas may be helpful:

Training leaders

The leaders of our children's groups should be encouraged to see their job as that of the 'pastor teacher', teaching the Bible in an age-appropriate, fun and stimulating way—we want children to be so excited about knowing Jesus that they're bringing mum and dad to church and not the other way round!

So we need to be praying for gifted men and women to be teaching our children and equipping them for the task. Regular training sessions are essential (why not take a chapter of this book as the subject matter for a session?) and of course we need to lovingly support our leaders by making sure they're getting fed, too.

Leaders need to be clear what the aim of each session is. How a session is put together will vary, but if leaders knew parents would be asking their children what they learned each time that would help them be more focused in their planning.

And they need to know their job isn't restricted to that one hour on a Sunday morning or whenever it may be. Leaders should be encouraged to take a genuine interest in the children's lives, asking what's going on at school, following up when they've missed a week or two, sending birthday cards, holding socials and, most of all, praying for them regularly. As we've said, parents are thrilled when others take an interest in their children's lives, yet for this to be properly understood, there needs to be good communication between parents and group leaders.

Training parents

Again, this will vary depending on the size of church, but Christian parents need to be taught as early as possible their spiritual responsibilities to their children. A special evening together with new parents may be a good time for this, or when speaking with parents about the baptism or thanksgiving for the new child. Or perhaps something before the baby is born might be more appropriate. Thinking about how such events could be turned into outreach opportunities can be very fruitful, since new parents can be more open to the gospel.

If leaders are preparing sessions, conscious that parents will be asking their children what they have learned, then parents obviously need to be trained to ask that question. This can be done in a number of different ways:

- **Parents' evenings:** If we have them for school, why not church?! Having an annual get-together over a drink and some nibbles for leaders to tell parents what their children have been learning, and for parents to ask questions, can be of great mutual encouragement. Without wanting to break confidences and undermine relationships, it can be helpful to hear from parents what the struggles are at that age, to allow programmes to be tailored more effectively.

- **Book evenings:** These can be an excellent excuse to meet with parents. Encouraging parents to read a relevant book, and getting together to discuss it, can lead to a great evening, bringing people together and helping them see they're not alone in their struggles as a Christian parent. You may not fully agree with everything in your chosen book, but this gives a great opportunity for further discussion. This has been done with *Teenagers—Why do they do that?* by Nick Pollard. It could also be done with *Fatherhood* by Tony Payne and many other good books*.

- **Time for God:** This is the name I gave to a Sunday afternoon training session that works well, but again depends on resources.

The model works as follows: Families are invited to church for a two-hour session. In one room games are set up (for example, bouncy castle, giant draughts, scalextric, arts 'n crafts etc.) and for the first half hour families enjoy them together. Then parents leave for some training while volunteers look after the children. Tea is served altogether for the last half an hour.

Encouraging parents to get together at least once a year for

---

* See the appendix on page 156 for further details.

training is an essential part of a healthy work among children and young people. In many ways, what is taught doesn't really matter, but ideas might include: 'How to pray with my children?'; 'Is my child a Christian?' etc.

Each time you bring parents together, you're reminding them of their responsibility to bring their children up to know and love the Lord Jesus for themselves and, conscious that most will be struggling, it's to be done in an atmosphere of great love and encouragement.

Special events as described above look impressive and will be of great help to parents. But, as is so often the case, it's the small things that count. So, when a friend asked recently how our Bible reading was going with our children, I came away thinking what a brilliant and loving question it was. It's not always an easy question to ask or be asked, but it reminds us as parents, and youth and children's workers, of the great privilege and responsibility we have to encourage one another to bring our children up to know the best Father of them all.

CASE STUDY
David and Penny have two children:
Isobel (6) and Richard (3)

This is what we currently do: Each morning, Penny will do some sort of brief, Bible-based activity with the children over breakfast: currently it's reading from the Lion Story Bible, but it could be a song or picture or memory verse or something topical. We also have a little photograph album with pictures of those for whom we regularly pray as a family, and we may use one of those photos to help us pray.

In the evening, both of us spend some time before the children go to bed reading the Bible with them individually and

---

praying before reading a bedtime story.

At weekends, we try to have a family time all together where we sing songs, pray and read the Bible all together, although pitching this can be difficult, because of the wide ability range of our children.

All this sounds excessive and a bit intense on paper but it isn't really. I guess there are times when any regular activity can become unthinkingly automatic, but when one of our children makes an unconscious, automatic connection between God's Word and an everyday life situation of some sort, then it's brilliant.

For us at present there are two big things to remember: first, to keep it varied. There are lots of different children's Bibles and resources available and we use a variety, including the standard 'Grown up's Bible'. There are also different ways to pray, and many songs to sing: yes, Colin Buchanan is great, but there lots of other good songs, too!

The second area is remembering to focus on what is godly rather than just 'respectable'. To tackle the second issue, we try to focus on teaching the Bible and apply it to our thinking, behaviour and understanding in everyday life. We try to show our children that God's Word is something we live by, rather than just teaching our own opinions or passing on a moral work. We need to show we're under the authority of God, too.

CASE STUDY
Sue and Simon have two children:
Becky (10) and Alex (7)

Sue is the more disciplined out of the two of us and started bedtime readings with Becky quite early on. For me it took a little time before the penny really dropped. Two things got me going. The first was an encouragement from a friend, that our children's Bible times should be just as part of their routines as washing their face and cleaning their teeth. The other came from the London Men's Convention when I was challenged to get going with Alex. Carl, our curate, then picked up the baton, saying that he would call me in a few weeks to see how we were getting on. This accountability really got me motivated and so Alex got his first quiet times.

BE REALISTIC: Of course, it doesn't always work. The important thing is not to get a guilt trip and not to pass that guilt trip onto the kids. If the habit has been broken—restart TODAY, try tomorrow and see how the rest of the week pans out. Life has its many distractions, some good some bad.

BE REWARDED: The rewards do come. One night, having put Alex to bed half an hour or so earlier, I went up to check on him only to find him reading his own Bible to himself. And in 2005 I helped baptise Becky. To say I was ecstatic was an understatement.

BE PRACTICAL: Get a Bible and notes that your children are happy with. It may not appeal to you, or be what you think is best, *but* if they are OK with it and it is good content *any* Bible reading has to be good.

Neither Sue nor I had Bible-reading parents so we had no example to follow when Becky and Alex came along. My hope is that both of our children will therefore have a better foundation to give to our grandchildren!

Bible Study

Read Deuteronomy 6

1. List God's promises of blessing for His people in these verses.

2. How do we receive this blessing, according to this passage?

3. Look at v 1-6 and 21-22. What do we need to know before we teach (v 7-8) and answer (v 20) our children?

4. According to verse 7, where is it OK to leave God out of family life?

5. Applying verses 8 and 9 practically, what might be the modern equivalent for a family today?

6. 'Impress' (v 7, NIV) suggests a mark or imprint left on a child. What do you think this is?

Richard Newman is married to Joy and they try hard (but often fail!) to practise what they preach with their three girls, Anna, Lucy and Emily. Previously Youth Pastor at Bishop Hannington Church, Hove, Richard is now working at Christ Church, Cambridge.

11. Getting excited!

How can we get our church leadership excited about children's and youth work?

WHY THIS CHAPTER MATTERS: If your church leaders are already excited about children's and youth work, understand your strategy and priorities, and are encouraging, prayerful and supportive, then thank God for them. You can use the suggestions in this chapter to make the most what you already have. But I suspect that there will be many of you who are not blessed with such leaders. If that's your situation, there are several good reasons why they should be enthusiastic about your work, and good reasons too why it's worth your effort to involve them.

Ownership
The Bible gives to church leaders the responsibility for what is taught in church. They are to 'guard the deposit' of the gospel (2 Timothy 1 v 14), and drive away error and falsehood from the flock (2 Peter 3 v 17). This overall responsibility cannot be confined to sermons, but extends to all the Word ministry in

the church—from words that proclaim truth (or error) in the congregational singing, to the syllabus for the two-year-olds in crèche. Godly leaders will be intensely interested in the quality of children's and youth work in church.

Prayer

Given that Christian ministry is a ministry of the Word and prayer, the leadership will want to pray in the most intelligent way possible for the youth work. As they do, this prayerfulness will filter down to the whole church, and the dependence of the work on God to work through His Word, (rather than the personalities of youth leaders, say) will be meaningfully shared.

Accountability

Church leaders should be able to use their experience and training to help youth leaders with critical evaluation of the work. Being accountable to an interested and informed leadership should keep you on your toes. It also means that if contentious issues arise (as they may when you change things), they are there to stand by you and fight your corner.

A shared strategy is an achievable strategy

This is the most important reason of all and is at the centre of most of this chapter. The successful youth and children's work will be part of the wider strategy of the local church. If the strategy is shared, both the whole church and the youth work should benefit.

This final reason for exciting the leadership about youth work is also the main *means* of doing it. A sharply gospel-focused strategy, based on biblical principles, cannot fail to excite a leadership that is similarly gospel focused and biblically minded.

However, there are other steps which complement this, which we will come to. And before you do anything, it would be wise to take a step back and think a little about your particular leaders.

Here then, are seven suggestions which, taken together, and carried out prayerfully and humbly, may under God see your leaders, and therefore your whole church, newly excited about ministry to children and young people.

1. Get to know the leaders

The title of this chapter doesn't necessarily imply that the leaders are against children's and youth work, but that they are simply not thinking about it productively—it's not 'on their radar'. Before you attempt to address the problem, it would be helpful to understand why this is the case. There can be several factors operating in the background.

Attitudes

A common attitude among busy leaders simply places this work low down on the scale of priorities. This might be exacerbated by ignorance, ('it's easy', 'it's just about telling stories'); or complacency, ('it's already happening', 'it's not my department'); or even fear ('I just don't know anything about children'). Occasionally, one comes across leaders who may be notorious control freaks in every other area of church life from the flower rota to the colour of the carpets, but who have never so much as glanced through the Sunday-school syllabus!

Assumptions

A common and tenaciously-held assumption is this: 'if you can see it, it's good'. That is, people will often be impressed by large numbers of kids simply 'in the building' on a Friday night, whether or not there is any decent biblical content to the programme; or by a large buzzing high-tech youth service, which looks great, but is devoid of follow-up, discipleship or Bible study, because all the leaders are too busy preparing *vox pop* videos and sketches for the event.

Perhaps this comes from an ungodly view of success, which focuses on numbers and programmes at the expense of the real hard work of making disciples through Bible teaching in small group and one-to-one settings.

Motives

Leaders may be keen to see children's and youth work happening for the wrong reasons. There are several widely-held beliefs which are rarely questioned. One is: 'We must reach children because they are the church of tomorrow'. True, but aren't they also the church of today? Couldn't you also argue that students or the thirty–somethings are the church of tomorrow?

Rather, isn't the primary motive because they are there, and they are sinful people who need the gospel—just like any other group? Being clear about this ought to raise the value of the work from the level of a human strategy to reach the next generation, to God's strategy for reaching every generation.

Another rarely questioned belief is: 'Reach the children in order to reach the parents'. This is a popular philosophy in churches where developing the fringe is the main evangelistic strategy. Contacts are made with parents by running mid-week children's clubs and holiday clubs. The problem is there is not a lot of evidence that it works, at least not in any way that repays the human resources taken up by doing it well. And it's a poor strategy in principle.

Since the Bible has plenty to say about parents—especially fathers—teaching children, and nothing to say about children teaching parents, wouldn't it be better to put our efforts into winning adults, especially men who, when converted, will then have a good chance of bringing along their wives and children too?

Presuppositions

The attitudes, assumptions and motives of the church leadership will help you to present your strategy sensitively and work out areas you'll need to emphasise. But you will want to make sure that you and the leadership share some basic presuppositions in regard to church and ministry in general, before you can proceed further.

For example, do you jointly believe:

- that the Bible is without error and contains all we need to know

- in the sinful nature of all people, including children of all ages

- in the need for faith in Jesus Christ for salvation

- in the primary responsibility of parents to teach children...

Fill out your own list.

2. Share the strategy

If the right presuppositions are in place, then you can build a biblical and convincing strategy that can be owned by the whole church.

Obviously, you'll have to work out the strategy for your own situation—for example, whether your main aim is to nurture the children of church families or to reach the non-Christian young people in the community. But a Bible-centred youth strategy would contain some essential elements:

- It will be dependent on the God-given tools of Word and prayer, rather than entertainment or personalities;

- It's aim will be discipleship of young people, not attracting a crowd;

- It will not separate evangelism from discipleship, but will rely on the gospel to bring people both to conversion and maturity and this will sharpen the focus of all the programmes you run.

Once you and your team have worked out a biblically driven strategy, the most important thing you can do now is to share it. This might mean visiting an elders' or church council meeting, speaking at an AGM or writing a discussion paper.

If none of these are possible, organise a one-off meeting to enable you to outline your vision. Invite the leaders of the church, along with all the youth team, and share the vision. Excite them about the potential for the gospel and prove it from the Bible. If the church leaders are gospel-minded, Bible-loving people, they cannot fail to be excited by such a strategy!

Don't be tempted to by-pass this step, as the benefits of a biblical strategy that is wholeheartedly owned by the leadership of a church are hard to overemphasise.

First: The youth work will be driven by, and assessed against, this strategy rather than other people's expectations. For example, if you are replacing an old programme which aimed to draw large numbers to high-profile events, with a biblical strategy aiming at discipleship by means of small-group Bible studies, numbers could well drop off initially and it could look from the outside like things are going downhill. You need the leaders on board to help explain to parents and church members why this is happening.

Secondly: A shared strategy will be able to recognise the place of the whole church in shaping the whole person. There are more contributing factors that shape a young person's spiritual development than what happens in youth group. After all, the Bible consistently lays the primary responsibility for teaching children on their parents. One implication of this for the church is that children's ministry will be seen as aiding parents in this role, not taking it from them. This kind of ethos can be best expressed by the church leaders. (See chapter 10, 'Bridging the gap', for more on this.)

Thirdly: A shared strategy helps with the tricky business of flow and integration—moving people from one part of church life to another as they become older, without losing them at the stages of transition. For example, if you care about the young people in your youth group, you will care as much about what happens to them when they leave at 18. What is there for them to go into that will help them grow? Is the next decent thing on the church programme the over 60's lunchtime club? You will want input into other areas of church life so that your work is not wasted.

Finally: When it comes to distributing the church's resources (money, staff, public air time, use of buildings etc.) the youth work will have a better chance of getting what is needed from a leadership who own the plans themselves. Being involved in this aspect of church life brings a healthy realism to youth leaders too. There is no point in running a fantastic youth programme, sucking in 80% of the church's resources, in a church where everything else is second rate because there is no one else and no money available to do anything.

3. Raise the profile

Once you have convinced others about your approach (and begun to implement it!) you need to keep things on the boil. So take some steps to deliberately raise the profile of youth and children's ministry in church.

- Invite leaders regularly to visit the various groups. Perhaps this can be formalised by establishing a link between each group and a church leader, who visits once or twice a year and then reports back to the other leaders.

- Why not formally 'commission' your Sunday school and youth leaders at the start of the year in a Sunday service? This reminds everyone of the seriousness of their task and the fact that they need our prayers as they teach the Bible.

- Organise some visits to other groups in the church family to update them on the work. Is there an old people's lunchtime group who you can ask to pray for you? If they are gospel-minded people they will love hearing about the work and praying for it and you'll be amazed how much 'prayer fodder' it will take to keep them going. Give it to them!

- Hold open events to show-case the groups that are best modelling what you are trying to do. Having worked through *The King, the Snake and the Promise*, our 3-6's and 7-11's after-school clubs put on a joint open event one evening at the end of term. Talking through the syllabus with songs, readings from children and a PowerPoint presentation served to show what had been happening at the club that term, to parents as well as church members and leaders. It is now a regular highlight of the church calendar.

- Get some regular air time at public meetings. If you are on the staff team of a church this is easy as you may be able to build it into services you are leading. If not, suggest it to those who do lead. The aim is to inform the church as to what is happening in the children's and youth work by using five minute slots, so they can be encouraged and pray more intelligently. Interview leaders of various groups or even children. Talk about the aims of the group and the benefits of what they are doing. If you have the expertise in your church, why not make a brief video and show it on a Sunday morning? Remember to be intentional about making the aims come across—so don't just show a bit of speeded up volley-ball, but get the young people talking about what they've learnt this term from Mark's Gospel.

- Make sure the service leader prays as children go out of the main meeting into their Sunday school. Even better, let him know what they will be learning that day so he can mention it, whetting the appetite of the children and encouraging families to discuss the subject over lunch.

- Produce a brochure outlining what happens in church for young people and include the biblical principles. Give a copy to every member and make it available for new people. Or, if you or someone in the church family has the ability, why not make a DVD with a sample of everything that happens in this part of church life—interviews with leaders, testimonies of children and so on.

- Communicate with parents. Send regular letters home outlining what the children are learning this term. Why not have some colourful fridge magnets made with the syllabus on?

Raising the profile like this is not an end in itself and is certainly not an opportunity to talk up your particular ministry for its own sake! Rather, it serves some very specific aims. Every time you speak or write about children's and youth work you have an opportunity to articulate the principles of the work, so that people are able to support and pray for it. You need to be intentional and repetitive about this in order for uninterested people to catch on.

Also, as people are reminded of the size and scale of the work, you will start to gain more volunteers without ever actually appealing directly for them.

4. Do one thing well

In some situations, organising and implementing a youth work strategy for the whole church will not be possible either because of time and man-power or because of rigid attitudes to change. Even for full-time youth workers it will be impossible to cover every aspect and every age at once.

Instead of spreading yourself too thin, choose one area or age group and specialise in that. Put most of your time and energy into one group, deliberately neglecting the rest for a while. Hold your nerve and get that one thing really good so it can operate as a model of what needs to be done elsewhere. After a while people will look over the fence, start to believe the strategy and want to adopt it for their own group.

5. Get a voice on the leadership

If you do not have a full-time member of staff responsible for youth work, you need to get some kind of youth and children's ministry 'advocate' on the leadership team. This person—perhaps an elder or member of the church council who is particularly interested—will champion the cause, keep other leaders informed and will provide feedback to you.

However, if you find yourself in the position of 'youth advocate' on a leadership team, do make sure you don't come across as a 'single-issue politician'—lobbying for youth issues at the expense of all else. For a start, if you yourself are a wise leader, you know that there is more to church than this. In addition, people will listen to your suggestions better against a backdrop of a rounded understanding of what the church is trying to achieve overall.

6. Make changes regularly

Change can be a very effective instrument to get people excited about things in church. I assume that in any gospel ministry we want to continually refine and improve what we are doing. But there are further benefits brought by change itself.

First, because of the human tendency to enshrine human structures with spiritual importance, changing those structures reminds us that the gospel is the only thing that never changes. This helps us keep our confidence in the gospel and not the human structures.

Secondly, every change provides a fresh opportunity to explain once again what you are doing and why, to both church and leadership. 'Could I grab ten minutes to explain the new 11-14's syllabus?' sounds better than 'Could I grab ten minutes to go over what I said last term again?'. You do the latter, of course, in the process of talking about the new syllabus!

7. Build in elements that serve the whole church

This is where you need to step back and look at what you are doing from the widest possible angle. We are not building empires or ministries which impress. As youth and children's leaders, we are servants of the gospel and are playing our part in the building of Jesus' church upwards and outwards (Ephesians 4 v 11-13).

If you have supportive, faithful leaders, give thanks to God that you are part of something exciting and make sure you reciprocate the encouragement. And despite the fact that sometimes this work is under-valued or misunderstood by others, we must avoid letting 'us and them' attitudes develop. Rather, we need to find creative ways in which youth and children's ministry serves the whole church. See the **Case Study** below for an example of this.

Like any ministry that holds out the offer of hope and forgiveness through Jesus Christ to sinful people, children's and youth ministry is inherently exciting and interesting. The task of motivating church leaders to be excited about it can only serve to increase the impact of the gospel on young people, and indeed the whole church, as many people rather than a few, start pulling the oars in the same direction so that the Lord Jesus is glorified.

CASE STUDY

A summer holiday club I was involved in serves as an example of building in elements of children's ministry that serve the whole church.

This particular holiday club became, over time, the biggest event on the church calendar and a huge drain on resources, using a significant amount of money and thousands of hours of work for the team of sixty adult leaders. Why justify this effort?

Well, one reason of course is that it was a great chance to share the gospel with unchurched children, many of whom would then join our clubs in September. A second reason was that it did give us a modest opportunity to make contacts

---

with non-Christian parents, who would then be invited to *Christianity Explored* groups in the autumn term. (Notice the purpose of the holiday club was not to 'get the children and get the adults'. Rather there was a conscious decision to make sure the holiday club served the existing adult evangelistic efforts.)

By far the biggest benefit of the club in our minds, however, was in training leaders. This was an integral part of the way the week was organised. For example, as well as every member of the team receiving some general training in the months before, the week itself was structured so that new leaders and older teenagers with obvious leadership potential were given the chance to prepare a talk for their group, along with a more experienced mentor to help them and provide feedback. The whole week served as an on-the-job training opportunity.

And the aim is wider than developing leaders for more children's work—the aim is to change people from being *willing helpers* to being *able servants*, people who have begun to develop a taste for gospel ministry, and to give them some basic tools that will last for a life-time of useful ministry in any area. In this way, something like a holiday club, which is a considerable cost to a church, can serve the whole church in providing able gospel workers for the future—and any leader ought to be excited about that!

Danny Rurlander is married to Emma and they have four children. He is the pastor of Moorlands Evangelical Church in Lancaster. He is also involved in training initiatives for children's and youth leaders in the North West. Danny enjoys good coffee, child-friendly walks in the Lake District and ticking things off to-do lists.

Bible Study

Read Colossians 1 v 24–29

1. What does Paul tell us about his own ministry—how it came to him and his experience in discharging it? (v 24–25a)

2. How does he describe the content of that ministry? (v 25b–28a)

3. What is the goal of the apostolic ministry? What is the method? (v 28)

4. Notice that the proclamation of Christ takes place in both negative and positive ways (admonishing and teaching). How does this work out in practice?

5. Describe in your own words Paul's commitment to this ministry? (v 29) What is his experience as he labours? How does this challenge and encourage us?

6. Think through the broader implications of Paul's goals and method for your children's and youth work:

   a. Do you have a clear biblical aim for the work: what is it?

   b. Is the work effectively directed towards this aim? Do some parts of the work detract from it?

   c. Do you and your team have confidence in the God-given means to accomplish the work?

   d. Does your strategy and programme use these means as effectively as possible? If not, what would be a better model?

Appendix

RECOMMENDED RESOURCES

Training opportunities:

- **The Big Issue** is an annual series of training days aimed at helping those involved with children and young people to do Bible-centred work that will equip young people to engage with the Bible for themselves and come to know God through it. Contact The Good Book Company* for further details.

- **The Bible-centred Youthworker** is a four-day conference, held each January, for full-time children's and youth workers. Contact The Good Book Company* for further details.

- **The Moore College Correspondence Course** is a distance learning course for anyone who wants to develop their understanding of the Bible. Full details by phoning 0845 225 0885 or at www.open-bible-institute.org.

---

* The Good Book Company 0845 225 0880 www.thegoodbook.co.uk

Books to help you understand a Bible passage and teach it faithfully:

- **Dig deeper** by Nigel Beynon and Andrew Sach (IVP, 2005).

- **How to read the Bible for all it's worth** by Gordon Fee and Douglas Stuart (Zondervan, 2003).

Resources to help you unfold the big story of the Bible:

- **God's Big Picture** by Vaughan Roberts (IVP, 2003).

- **Gospel and Kingdom** by Graeme Goldsworthy (available as part of **The Goldsworthy Trilogy**, Paternoster, 2000).

- **The King, the Snake and the Promise**: an enhanced CD Rom that contains teaching material for 5-11s, to teach a Bible overview in ten sessions, plus 29 songs (Emu Music, 1998, available from The Good Book Company*).

- **Out of this world** by Nick Jones (part of the **Lightning Bolts** series, Bible Reading Fellowship, 1995).

- **Teaching little ones**: a range of teaching material for under 8s. Available from The Good Book Company* or from the website www.teachinglittleones.com.

- **CLICK**: the syllabus for the CLICK teaching material for 3-11s is based round the Bible's own theological framework. Available from The Good Book Company*.

- **Bible timelines**: a set of full-colour A2 posters to create a Bible timeline (published by CEP) is available from The Good Book Company*. A mini Bible timeline, initially designed to support XTB Bible reading notes for 8-11s, is also available from The Good Book Company.

---

* The Good Book Company 0845 225 0880 www.thegoodbook.co.uk

Resources to help families and young people read the Bible:

- **Table Talk**: Bible-reading notes for families
- **Advent Calendar Pack**: an Advent calendar with accompanying booklet to help families read the Bible together during Advent
- **XTB (eXplore The Bible)**: Bible-reading notes for children
- **Discover**: Bible-reading notes for 11-14s

These resources are all available from The Good Book Company*

Books for parents:

- **Fatherhood—what it is and what it's for** by Tony Payne (Matthias Media, 2004, available from The Good Book Company*)
- **Teenagers: why do they do that?** by Nick Pollard (Damaris Books, 2006)

---

* The Good Book Company 0845 225 0880 www.thegoodbook.co.uk